A Secret van Gogh

His Motif and Motives

Antonino Saggio

*To Caterina
perché difenda il giusto*

Published in March 2011

Second Edition July 2011

ISBN 978-1-4475-0793-2

Copy of this book can be ordered or downloaded at
http://stores.lulu.com/ninos or http://www.amazon.com/

Italian edition, *Van Gogh Segreto,* Edizioni Kappa, Roma 2011

Translated from Italian
by Rebecca Guarda
www.rebeccaguarda.com/

Special Thanks to
Glenn Boornazian and Mrs Loretta Schaeffer

Books by this Author:

L'opera di Giuseppe Pagano tra politica e architettura (Dedalo, 1984)
Using Goals in Design (CMU, 1988)
Giuseppe Terragni. Vita e opere (Laterza, 2005^3)
Peter Eisenman. Trivellazioni nel futuro (Testo&Immagine, 1996)
Frank Gehry. Architetture residuali (Testo&Immagine, 1997)
The Instrument of Caravaggio (Kappa, 2007)
The IT Revolution in Architecture. Thoughts on a Paradigm Shift (Carocci, 2007, Lulu, 2009)
Five Masterworks by Louis Sauer (Lulu, 2010)
Architettura e modernità. Dal Bauhaus alla rivoluzione informatica (Carocci, 2010)

p. 1

Walking Couple, «The Lovers», Arles, c. March 16,1888 Private Collection, 23x32,5 F 544

Back cover

Vincent's Bedroom, «For the Mother», Saint Rémy, c. September 18, 1889 Museum d'Orsay, Paris, 56.5x74 F 483

Cover

Couple Walking with a Crescent Moon, Saint-Rémy, c. May 18, 1890 Museum of Art, San Paolo, 45.5x49,5 F 704

CONTENTS

7 *Introduction*
8 *The Bible*
12 *Vincents*
13 *The Shoes*
15 *The Wait*
16 *The Tunnel*
20 *«Souvenir de Mauve»*
22 *Sunflowers and Vincent's Bedroom*
27 *Paul & Vincent Alone*
28 *The Gardener's Eyes*
33 *The Sun of the Night*
38 *Addendum*
45 *The Inquiry*

    46 *Gauguin and Theo's role*
    49 *The Reality of Life*
    51 *Iman, Rachel and the Secrets of the Bedroom*
    53 *The Razor Blade*

57 *Icons*
58 *Flowers*
63 *Chronology of Events*
67 *Annotated Bibliography*
64 *Endnotes*

Self-portrait dedicated to Paul Gauguin, «The Bonze», Arles c. September 16, 1888, Fogg Art Museum, Harvard University, Cambridge, MA, USA, 62x52 F 476

A Secret van Gogh

I have made my decision by now. My despair weighs too much upon me and I have lost hope of finding love. All is lost without love.

I am at peace with my decision. I imagine that at the moment of death, I shall perceive the world superimposed and clear, and, at that instant, all shall be serene.

I will see many quickly spinning visions. I will see my Mother with her colors, you and the girls among the garden trees and myself hunting for frogs. I will see my Father and the cemetery tower that always appeared about to speak. I will see you brother, with your wife and baby Vincent, happy together.

It is a short while now that I have been thinking of this. I believe this the only and best option for us all.

I pondered this moment of departure and of death and I perceive it as a horizontal shift, where one returns to mother earth.

You will find these last works long and narrow.
One of wheat beneath a storm, one of crows and one of tree roots that nourish themselves of the soil.
The last is not a pretty painting, but what I was searching to express will become evident to you. To the earth, we return and from the earth, new life emerges and grows. The earth, the earth.
I imagine that before dying, the very instant before my death, I shall recall the pit of Borinage. Remember when I wrote to you of those long descents with the miners into the hells of 300, 400, 500, 600 meter depths, lower and lower! As I descended, the light above me grew ever smaller, a well, a dimming flame, a dying star.
My star is darkened now.
I see my sunflowers, my paintings, my room in the suddenness of a flash. I see my loves all together in my last bedroom at Arles. Unhappy loves. Love, lonely and tragic but to which I desperately clung. It felt right to pursue my dream that as a painter, no matter my eccentricities, I could find love. I tried and I struggled toward this dream. I fought to attain this when I was interned in Saint Rémy. I fought desperately not to extinguish my heart. But now is the time for an end.
I risked it all for my works and burned up my life in them, for which I pray it served.[1]

Introduction

This book seeks to provide a tangible key for unlocking the meaning behind Vincent van Gogh's works. It is a rather unexplored interpretation, despite some small clues contained in the writings of two Italian scholars. The reader will also discover a layering of different writing styles, unusual for scholarly writing, but more likened to life and thought itself. Through this layering technique, the reader can imagine himself within the very works of van Gogh and re-evaluate them from that point of view.

There is also a biographical element interlaced in the text that has enthralled the first readers of the manuscript. It is the inquiry, from incontrovertible sources, of a key episode in van Gogh's life; on the other side, is not the world "Inquiry" a good clarification of the true meaning of "History" itself?[2] The specific episode is the amputation of the ear in Arles along with the actors involved in the event. A new interpretation is explored of which I hope to convince the reader.

Lastly, important clues regarding the painter's intimate and emotional state are hidden inside the details of his paintings. I focus on these at length in the final part of the book.

Reproductions were selected from the dozens available in print and on the internet that were most faithful to the original. I am greatly indebted to the generous collectors, foundations and museums that share the many works of the artist and related research with the public. I am particularly grateful to the van Gogh Museum in Amsterdam for the vast array of information it makes available through print and on the web in support of scholarly research. The «Chronology of Events» (see pp. 63-65) is annotated to have a more precise understanding of the circumstances of Vincent's life, the «Endnotes» section is quite extensive with detailed bibliographical and archival support for the different aspect of the book's thesis. The «Annotated Bibliography» (see pp. 67-70) provides a useful resource to the reader for further research of relevant texts.

Vincent's handwriting is used in the typesetting of this book in two cases. In one case, there are letters written by Vincent van Gogh. In the other case, there are "possible" letters that are of my own composition with footnote stating that the letters do not exist but are can be considered plausible.

The Bible

How does one begin to describe the violent and beautiful force of Vincent van Gogh? The answer is a terrible tangled and interlaced knot of motives. A key to his origins is needed in order to begin to untangle this knot. I believe, to enter his world, one must start with STILL LIFE WITH BIBLE, painted at his father's death. Let us reconstruct the scene.

Vincent comes from a Dutch middle-class family. The prevalent trades of the family are either pastor or art dealer. (His brother Theo, from age 23 onward, becomes the director of a major French art dealership). Vincent - who has an active correspondence with Theo since their teens - will try both trades as a young man. At first, for some years, he is an apprentice art dealer in London, Paris and the Hague. He abandons this work for a passionate study of theology so as to become an ordained pastor. However, he never takes his final exams nor becomes ordained. He then lives two impoverished years as an unpaid evangelist among destitute minors in Belgium. At the young age of 27, he suffers a traumatic religious crisis, abandons his preaching and decides to become a painter. He zealously pursues this new endeavor through a self-taught process.

For the next two years he resides at the Hague with a prostitute and spends his time sketching her as well as the poor in the area. He then returns home to Nuenen, a barren and remote village in the South of Holland. There he lives in a small annex, the former home of the village sexton, inside his father the vicar's garden. Vincent paints and draws with extraordinary tenacity. Extremely powerful works emerge. The subjects are humble workers of the earth, portraits of faces stained with mud which appear to be carved in wood with the same roughness of the very clogs they wear; their bodies are inexorably bent by their labor.

He signs a contract with Theo. In exchange for a small monthly stipend, all his works will be Theo's property who, in turn, will try to sell them. It is a professional agreement between two men, both already well acquainted with the field of art.

He has bitter arguments with his father. Opposing natures clash. The father is conservative, rigid and puritan, burdened by the meager economy in their isolated farming village. The son is an artist, extreme and eccentric. He wears a fur cap and a traditional worker's blue shirt made with the same cloth of Genovese sailor's garb, the antecedent of jeans.

Peasant Woman Stooping and Gleaning, Nuenen, July 1885, Museum Folkwang, Essen, 41,5x51,5 F 1279

10. *Still Life with Bible*, Nuenen, October 1885, van Gogh Museum, Amsterdam, 65x78 F 117

Brother's tomb, deceased on March 30, 1852, Cemetery of Zundert, Tralbaut 1970

Honesty in a vase, Nuenen, Sketch in the letter to Theo of April 6, 1885, 13x21 JH 726

Let us return to STILL LIFE WITH BIBLE of 1885. Observe it carefully and one grasps the first piece of the key.

A huge and gigantic Bible emerges from the darkness. There is also a smaller yellow book and a candlestick with a melted stub. Looming above the secondary objects is "it", the Bible. The book seems to practically jump out of the canvas, to recite, to want to speak.

This sensation of an object becoming alive is a characteristic that, I believe, seizes all viewers of a van Gogh. The Bible goes beyond being a simple still-life object to become a living thing, an expression of strength, an existence that emanates from itself, beyond the painting surface to participate in our very lives.

> What van Gogh seeks is a painting so real as to reach the absurd; alive to the point of frenzy, delirium, death. The materiality of the paint takes on an, exasperated, almost unbearable independence: the painting is no longer a representation; it simply becomes.[3]

This painting, therefore, is not just a "still life". It is the portrait of a father whom Vincent had never portrayed, but whose personality seems to emerge from the painting and possess the bystander. It is an incredible still life, so still that it becomes hyper alive. This is the crux of the battle van Gogh engages with objects, how to depict the inanimate vs. nature and yet also render the object alive and psychologically vibrant.

I believe this 1885 painting is one of the very first in which Van Gogh's motif of personification emerges. It is a recurring theme of intimate contradictions. We can interpret Cézanne as a painter who strives to reduce everything to the object. Indeed, he analytically de-constructs the objects of his paintings in an "analysis" of the object (apples, mountains, bathing nudes).[4] Van Gogh uses an opposite approach: how to transform everything, into "being"? How does one reveal the everything of creation with the dramatic and vanishing power of life? He does not simply render an object but, on the contrary, imbues the object with a human being-ness.

This idea brings up a second question. If the objects we paint are rendered alive then, they speak to us simultaneously of our own selves which created them in our own image. We transfigure them into signifiers of our hopes, dreams and fears.

STILL LIFE WITH BIBLE underscores this complex psychological layer. Van Gogh painted this picture as if his father's presence were felt; laying in the very next room.[5] In the composition, Vincent includes a metaphorical portrait of himself as the smaller yellow novel. It is Émile Zola's *La Joie de Vivre* which, from the pastor father's point of view, is a scandalous and obscene modern book. Its protagonist explores her sensuality and, despite being burdened with multiple misfortunes, will not give up on her desire to live life fully. The painting reveals van Gogh's similar determination to never yield up his beliefs. This is a given constant of his character: he juxtaposes before his father's very Bible his own belief system in the form of *The Joy of Life*.[6]

This intense search for life in inanimate objects is closely linked with its opposite: death itself. The interjection of death as a subject is an integral characteristic of a van Gogh and it can also be traced back to his personal biography.

Vincents

Vincent Willem van Gogh was born on March 30, 1853, in Zundert, located in the Brabant southern region of the Netherlands. He was the firstborn of six brothers and sisters. The cemetery in Holland lies adjacent to the church, which in turn is attached to the village pastor's home. This forms a unique ensemble: church, garden, cemetery, house; house-cemetery-church; church-garden-house... cemetery. At what age did Vincent discover the object that would haunt him for life? At six years of age... when he had just begun to read? At seven, when he hunted for bird nests, herbs or fallen fledglings?

The Old Church, «The Tower of the Cemetery», Nuenen, May 1884, Foundation E.G. Bührle, Zürich, 47,5x55 F 88

He discovered a tombstone in this cemetery. «Vincent van Gogh, 1852» was inscribed on it along with a few lines from the Bible. If that tombstone carries my name, is it me? Am I dead or am I alive? Who is Vincent? Is it me or am I buried beneath that marble slab?

Perhaps the discovery of his brother's tombstone; who was born and died exactly one year prior to his very own birth, marked his life with a fear of death. In his case, it was emphatically announced as if it had already happened. Death becomes intimately connected to his own life and objects become intimately linked to life. This tombstone is not simply a sign of afterlife, but becomes itself alive, given that I exist. I who shares the same name now stand alive.[7] Here emerges a desperate necessity; I can only exist if I give life to what surrounds me.

Van Gogh paints in Nuenen at least five oil paintings along with many drawings and sketches of the cemetery tower. Let us turn now to the work in Zurich that he painted in 1884 of THE OLD CHURCH TOWER at Nuenen. The tombstone crosses are shown low, where his father is buried. The flat landscape is desolate; shrouded in mist from which the tower emerges. It stands alone, presaging death, but also a living type of death, a goodbye that does not extinguish beingness, a death that speaks.[8]

He gifts the painting to Margot Begemann, as if it were a self portrait, and leaves for Anvers. By the end of February 1886, he lands in Paris.

The Shoes

Vincent paints six canvases of his work boots during his time in Paris. They are rough and worn with heavily nailed soles. Each mark, fold and wrinkle relates a story. The shoes themselves epitomize the memory of time. One could reconstruct the events of a life by studying and scrutinizing their every fold.

He paints with Émile Bernard at times. Bernard is a young painter known in Parisian studio circles which he formerly frequented. He is very talented, with vision, passion and a fondness for Vincent who reciprocates the friendship. At other times, Vincent paints with Paul Signac along the river at Asnières-sur-Seine.

He often paints the new outskirts of Paris or Asnières. His subjects are in the fringes where the city grows and invades the countryside, where islands of nature

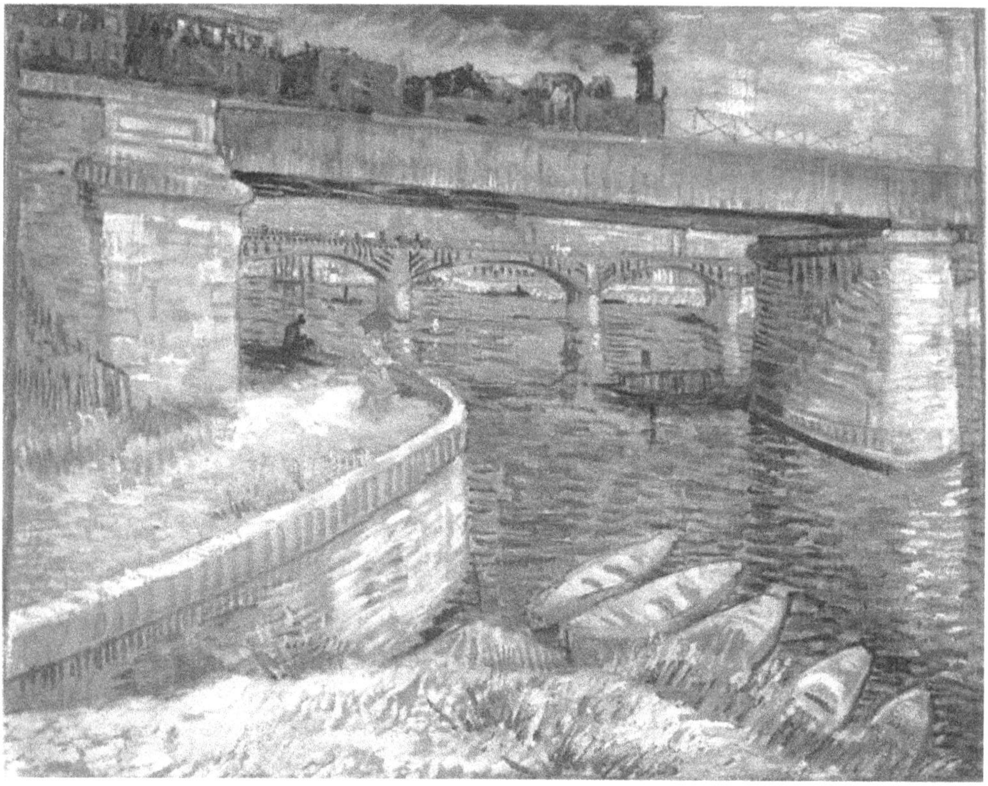

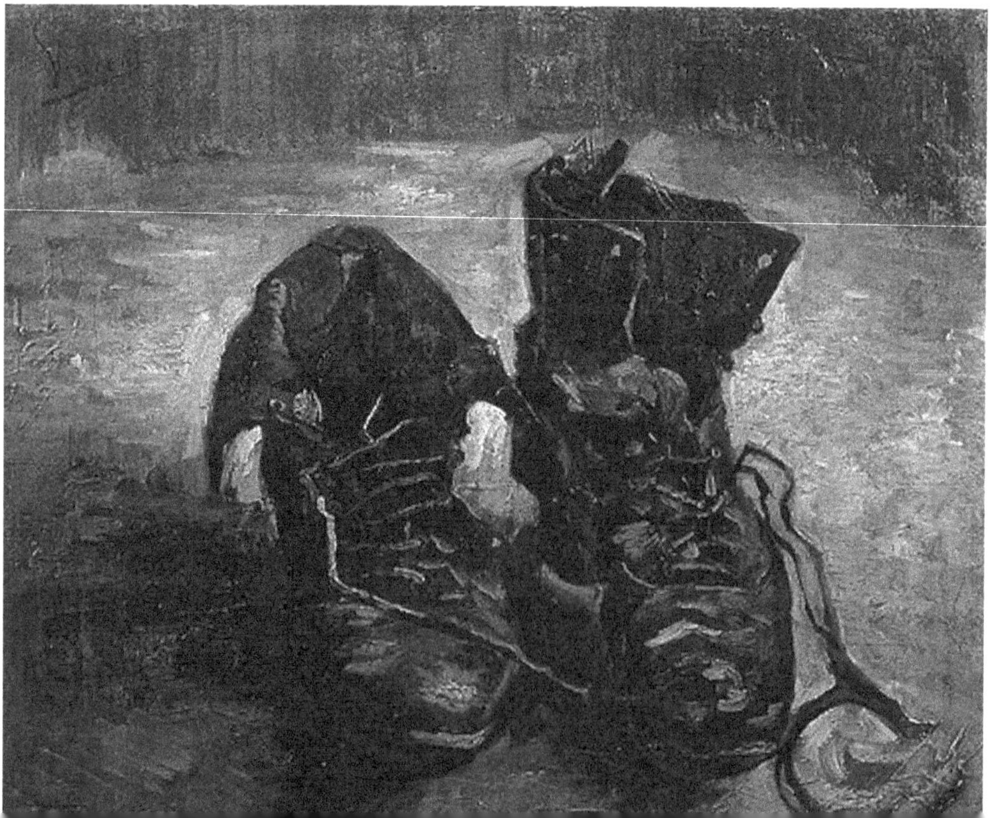

coexist with new buildings, where new smoke stacks contrast with fields of brambles and where the bridges carry the sounds of the trains.In the morning he heads out with a large canvas, wearing the same shoes that have replaced his Dutch clogs. [9] He will later divide the canvas up and return in the evening with three, four, five or six painting studies. His shoes become his means for wandering. They symbolize that he is a worker, a painter and perhaps also allude to his relationship to Theo. The shoes are often depicted with a lace connecting the pair, a symbol of the tie between the brothers (Tralbaut 1969).

Theo is busy with management of his branch at Boussod&Valadon, a well established art dealership. Vincent creates and shares with Theo a circle of friends among new painters. An opportunity emerges for Theo to represent them and open a new art market. Paul Gauguin, Henri Toulouse Lautrec, Lucien Pissarro, Luis Anquetin, Charles Angrand, Arnold Koning, Armand Guillaumin. Paul Seurat, Bernard, Signac are Petit Boulevard painters looking for new space to show their work in that it is an alternative to the already established first generation of Impressionists (Manet, Monet, Renoir, Degas). Theo, in the meantime, is beginning to sell well the established Impressionists in the Grand Boulevard, near Montmartre where his dealership branch is headquartered. Vincent also organizes small painting exhibits in the socialist père Tanguy's art supply store as well as in small restaurants and cafes. His effort to showcase the popular Japanese woodcut print form creates a particularly important exhibit. The prints are not simply an exotic fashion but a lasting inspiration for both van Gogh and the painters of the Petit Boulevard. That colorful, flat and graphic world re-defines perspective and opens up new visual possibilities for artists to explore.

The Wait

In this creative climate, he paints INTERIOR OF A RESTAURANT showing tables decorated with flowers. An initial reading of the painting offers no ulterior motives or clarifying hints as to the exact place or scenario.[10] The simplicity of the title suggests just a restaurant and nothing more but, if one examines it further, a series of revelatory details emerge.

Bridge across the Seine at Asnières, Summer 1887, Foundation E.G. Bührle, Zürich, 52x65 F 301

A Pair of Shoes, Paris, December 1886, van Gogh Museum, Amsterdam, 37,5x45,5 F 255

The 1887 painting is made at the time in which Vincent is an active participant in the Paris art scene. A poster on the wall could be the exhibition announcement for the Japanese prints that van Gogh organized or, it may simply be an invitation to another show. The tables are set for a simple luncheon; however, they are exuberantly decorated. Each table has a vase filled with flowers of such grandeur and beauty that a marked contrast is made between them and the modest wooden and straw chairs. By this time in Paris, Van Gogh has painted dozens of still lifes with flowers; always choosing carefully what to paint and at times personally visiting the florist. In this interior, the care given to the vases, the grandeur and variety of the flower arrangements makes one think of a painter's care for the details of decoration. The picture in the center of the wall has both subject matter and impressionist colors and may be from the very same series van Gogh painted at Asnières. If one looks in the upper corner, one also sees a cylindrical hat. This hat, hanging on a hook, suggests a moment of suspended judgement. Could it belong to the authoritative art critic Félix Fénéon, and thus become the device that makes him present to discuss the work with Vincent?

In short, the restaurant awaits an audience that is most likely there to celebrate a painting exhibition. In November 1887, Van Gogh effectively organized an exhibition of his friends from the Petit Boulevard and it was situated in a restaurant in Montmartre. It is quite possible that this painting represents precisely this restaurant: the Grand Bouillon-Restaurant du Chalet at 43 Av. de Clichy. In any case, the festive decoration indicates the approach of a celebration. The painting should have a date of November 1887 which is just when the exhibition opening occurred.[11]

The work itself is the most important in the end. Van Gogh shows no hesitancy here. He is clearly a painter of the new Pointilist avant-garde. He is well versed in the color theories that form its base and he enhances this knowledge with the use of complementary colors.

The Tunnel

The end of his Paris stay, however, culminates in a downward spiral. Beginning with the Summer of 1887 through to his departure for the South in February 1888,

Interior of a Restaurant with Flowers, «The Wait», Paris, c. November 1887, Kröller Müller Museum, Otterlo, 45,5x56,5 F 342

Vincent with art critic Félix Fénéon, Drawing by Lucien Pissarro, Paris, 1887 in Tralbaut 1969 p. 212

Vincent describes himself as semi-alcoholic, ill-mannered, depressed and angry. [12]

The painting Roadway with Underpass captures this state of mind. First of all, it is a symbolic subject; a tunnel. The painter is interested, as he has been in previous series, in the arrival to the outskirts of the city's industrial landscape. An even stronger character however emerges from this theme in the painting. This tunnel shares a history with his own past when Vincent lived among the miners of Borinage. He knows well what it means to be "physically" in a tunnel and not just psychologically.

The painter puts an iconic figure in the frame; a woman, dressed in black that he literally paints inside the tunnel, centered; at its darkest part.

These are the months after his break-up with Agostina Segatori. Agostina is of Italian origin, a dozen years older than Vincent and a beautiful model of many important painters. She manages the café in Montmartre with the tables shaped like drums in which van Gogh organized his February exhibition of Japanese prints. Vincent is romantically linked to her and painted her portrait at least three times, of which at least one was a nude. [13]

Now his relationship with Agostina, who possibly aborted his child, is over. She is the woman in the tunnel and she is ailing. Vincent buries himself in alcohol. The paintings he gave Agostina of flowers, that were used to decorated the cafe, are now sold at the the bankruptcy auction of Tambourin. There is no solution to this story even if he senses that there must be another way, another possibility. This underpass opens to an arch of light with a building's chimney stacks rising from the other side of the viaduct. It is a forced perspective, a pure abstraction and a clear sign that there may exist another way. In July o1887 he writes to Theo:

> Myself - I feel I'm losing the desire for marriage and children, and at times I'm quite melancholy to be like that at 35 when I ought to feel quite differently. And sometimes I blame this damned painting. It was Richepin who said somewhere: the love of art makes us lose real love. I find that terribly true, but on the other hand real love puts you right off art. And sometimes I already feel old and broken, but still sufficiently in

Roadway with Underpass, «The Tunnel», Paris, c. July 1887, Guggenheim Museum, New York, 31.5x40,5 F 239

love to stop me being enthusiastic about paintings[...] And then I'm going to retreat to somewhere in the south so as not to see so many painters who repel me as men.

You can be sure of one thing, and that's that I won't try to do any more work for the Tambourin. I think it's going to change hands, too, and of course I'm not against that.

As far as Miss Segatori is concerned, that's another matter altogether, I still feel affection for her and I hope she still feels some for me.

But now she's in an awkward position, she's neither free nor mistress in her own house, and most of all, she's sick and ill. Although I wouldn't say so in public - I'm personally convinced she's had an abortion (unless of course she had a miscarriage) - whatever the case, in her situation I wouldn't blame her. In two months she'll be better, I hope, and then perhaps she'll be grateful that I didn't bother her.[14]

Paris now tires and wears him down. His relationship with Agostina, ends. Many friends are also leaving and Vincent, perhaps following Lautrec's advice, departs. The Midi awaits him. It will be a magical south, incredible and completely new to a northerner like Vincent.

«Souvenir de Mauve»

Van Gogh abandons the dark tunnel of Paris in which he was trapped and makes a prodigious leap to the South of France. He arrives at Arles in Provence, during February, and is surprised to find snow. Gradually the days become longer, the snow melts and one after another, the orchards start blooming. What beauty! Vincent is speechless. He has always had an avid naturalist's passion for the phenomena of the earth. As a child he collected insects and nature holds a magical presence for him. This awakening of the trees amidst the bright sun of the Mediterranean spring is unknown to him. It spurs him to create an extraordinary series of canvases in quantity, quality and gaiety. It is unbelievable that after the darkness of Paris, such an awakening arrives. It does arrive, however, and along with it comes a whole new way of being and in this enlightened state he creates a sublime painting. He portrays two trees in an orchard with intertwined branches. The first is in the foreground with the second close behind, enveloping the former. The painting is significant. It is a mirror reflecting the painter who previously identified himself with the old lone tower of his town cemetery.

It is in a full colorful bloom, in an unforgettable light that will be recalled by any viewer when they encounter such a tree in bloom. The whites are startling, reds subtle, the greens and blues of the trunks stand out beneath an azure sky and reverberate their happy colors in the shadows on the ground.

Vincent receives a letter informing him of the death of hi cousinAnton Mauve. Schcked by the death, Vincent writes on this painting «Reminiscence of Mauve». What a gesture, what courage, what a marvel! Anton Mauve was his painter cousin in the Hague. He was an accomplished artist, sensitive and respected and yet, fifty years behind the times. Mauve was also a friend of their uncle Cent, an established member of the powerful Goupil Art Collective. When Vincent decides to become a painter, it is Mauve who gives him his first colors and painting lessons at the Hague. At that same time, Vincent starts using the model Sien. She is a destitute and unhappy woman; abandoned by God and men. After a few months, Vincent has her come reside with him along with her daughter and soon to be born child. The scandal this raises in the van Gogh family is enormous. The father takes offense, the admiral uncle is furious, his uncle Vincent disinherits him and Anton Mauve, the middle class painter, gives him an ultimatum: choose either him or the prostitute.

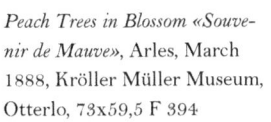

Peach Trees in Blossom «Souvenir de Mauve», Arles, March 1888, Kröller Müller Museum, Otterlo, 73x59,5 F 394

Peach Trees in Blossom, Arles, April 1888, van Gogh Museum, Amsterdam 40,5x30,5 F 1469

Orchard in Blossom, Arles, April 1888, Kröller Müller Museum, Otterlo, 65x81 F 513

21.

Vincent chooses Sien. Vincent chooses the side of pain, of the unhappy and of those who suffer. However now Mauve is dead, Vincent is happier than he has ever been. He writes this phrase and sends the painting to Mauve's widow. Death distances past wrongs and helps preserve the best memories. «Souvenir de Mauve».

Sunflowers and Vincent's Bedroom

Let's jump now to a moment of exaltation, of almost pure happiness. Two years have passed since the painting of the Paris boots, (only two years, but they could be a hundred). Van Gogh has succeeded at an incredible enterprise. He has rented a house at Arles. It is the little Yellow House (see p. 43), as he calls it. It all seems a dream come true. He wants to create a community of artists that can live together and at the same time sell their artwork as a cooperative. His idea had been studied in detail and repeatedly described to Theo. It has its origins among French landscape painters of the Barbizon School of the mid nineteenth century. Another contemporary example is set by his painter friends who are living together in Brittany. In order to start the project, van Gogh manages to initiate a trade agreement between the recalcitrant Paul Gauguin and Theo. Vincent feverishly awaits Gauguin who should become the Atelier's mentor. Van Gogh decides to decorate the house with a series of paintings of enormous sunflowers. He paints four canvases between August and September of 1888.

Have you ever seen the paintings of these sunflowers, especially the most powerful and beautiful one in the National Gallery of London? (It is well worth the trip). Once you have seen these sunflowers you understand what I am speaking of. The sunflowers are alive, powerful, overflowing with energy and bursting forth. They are happy in themselves; a literal chorus of welcome and homage.

The dazzling shapes of color are layered of tone upon tone. One, two, five... a thousand yellows. Van Gogh sets up a chrome yellow background and advances to the golden yellow petals, to the ochre bulbs textured in relief. Powerful form contrasts with the singularity of detail... leafs, petals, stems, seeds and seedless pockets of a naturalist's eye. The absence of perspective is simultaneously explored with a Japanese sensibility. It is as if this manifestation of life were to emanate from the stained glass of cathedral windows and the transformed sunflowers are life itself, saints and resurrected martyrs.

Sunflowers, Arles, c. August 20, 1888, National Gallery, London, 73x93 F 554

In short, van Gogh calls forth some absolutes in Art. Aesthetic vision comes from the liberal combination of disparate subjects resulting in unexpected and unpredictable associations; much as what happens in dreams. This vision begins via an unimaginable departure and renders the creative act a solution to a problem previously unknown to the artist. These sunflowers as such become living beings announcing Gauguin's arrival. Like ancient and primitive art, they contain within themselves the magical augury of the benign event. As we previously noted, another layer also exists. The objects become mirrors of ourselves. The bedroom Vincent depicts is in the same state of waiting as the sunflowers are a symbol. The bedroom is his self-portrait, the objects "are" the painter. The bed with its rustic wood, the bedcover, the urn, the mirror, the towel, the portraits of friends along the walls and the chairs create a community. Festive and ready for a new life to animate the setting. These objects are alive and at the same time infuse life into a thrilling and exalted circular dynamic.[15]

The Bedroom, Arles, c. 17 October, 1888, van Gogh Museum, Amsterdam 70x92 F 482

The painting of Vincent's bedroom underlines his effort to portrait a safe haven but it also hides an important clue. That summer he has repeatedly painted garden landscapes that often included a pair of lovers, with titles that had romantic references (see p. 79). This motif can be traced in his letters as well:

> A weaver, a basket-maker, often spends entire seasons alone, or almost alone, with his work as his only pastime.
> But what makes those people stay where they are is precisely the feeling of the house, the reassuring, familiar look of things. Of course I'd like company, but if I don't have it I won't be unhappy on that account, and then, above all, the time will come when I'll have someone. I have little doubt about that.
> [...] I'm beginning now to see better the beauty of the women here, [...] I believe that the town of Arles was once infinitely more glorious for the beauty of its women, [...] Milliet's lucky, he has all the Arlésiennes he wants, but there you are, he can't paint them, and if he was a painter he wouldn't have any.. I must bide my time now, without rushing anything.[16] [...and three days later] I have a lover's lucidity or blindness for work just now.[17]

Everything is doubled in the room: two pillows, two paintings, two drawings and two chairs: «I must bide my time now, without rushing anything, ... I have a lover's lucidity or blindness». In short, a multitude of clues converge in this bedroom of hope and expectation. We have here a masterpiece, from our inheritance of his works, in which van Gogh lucidly pursues the motif of Waiting.

Two months later van Gogh creates a pair of paintings, that are as much human portraits as they are the semblance of a chair.

Vincent's Chair with his Pipe, Arles, c. November 15, 1888, National Gallery, London, 73x93,5 F 498

Paul & Vincent Alone

Van Gogh has painted more than thirty self-portraits that measure his self-perception through a complex interplay between one's inner self, existing in the outer world, and the struggles of the interior vs. the exterior of one's being. There are dark and brooding portraits immersed in the lonesome light made in Antwerp, are bourgeois portraits of himself with a hat and tie in Paris and also those of him at work with a straw hat, his pipe and easel upon his shoulders. Then are there also the very last tormented ones where he appears withdrawn into himself away from a world spinning without reference.

Of all these portraits, perhaps Vincent's Chair with his Pipe is the most revealing. This chair is shown alone, desperately alone. Its presence occupies an unreal space where the floor tiles appear to rise up. In a box are onion or perhaps sunflower bulbs; the memory of another season now abandoned and left to themselves. The vivid chrome yellow color exudes a feeling of tension. Other objects evoke the author, like the tobacco paper and the pipe resting on the chair. The atmosphere is one of extreme solitude. The chair itself bursts from the frame in the same manner of the sunflowers two months earlier. But it screams out to relieve the built-up pressure it has endured. What is the reason for this tension?

Tension has accumulated during the recent months Vincent and Gauguin have been together in Arles. These are fascinating but hard months of hopes and burning disappointments. Van Gogh welcomes his friend to the house set up as the outpost of the artist colony he hopes to host in the Midi. Van Gogh admires Monticelli (a painter from Provence), he adores Millet, and understands Courbet. Instead Gauguin admires Rafael and Ingres... "Ingres? How is this possible?" thinks Vincent. "What could be further from Millet, Monticelli or Delacroix?" The reason for the difference is simple; Gauguin believes in a freedom in painting, this freedom being first and foremost an affirmation of the pure values of color and shape and not of the referential. «Vision of the Sermon» is perhaps the most important work Gauguin painted just before leaving for Arles. It depicts country girls listening to a priest in a unreal landscape. The young women, the priest and Jacob wrestling with the angel are all shown simultaneously in a scene where dreams and reality coexist. It is neither the sermon's story nor the reality of the country life that matters but rather, the willful pursuit of arbitrary juxtapositions of forms and compositions. If anything, this arbitrariness prolongs the image as a magical dream, but its method is quite different from that of van Gogh's.

Objects for Gauguin are de-personalized, stripped of their life and employed almost as decorative effigies.. In this manner he deceives the simple and the naive. Two opposing worlds, opposing loves, opposing natures collide progressively in the ensuing nine weeks of living together. Gauguin depicts van Gogh as he paints his sunflowers and van Gogh says: "yes, it is me...but as a madman". The portrait is the distillation of a trance. Gauguin is an equally great artist, talented and original and integral to the History of art, but his cynicism toward people and ideas will inevitably conflict with van Gogh's desperation of being.

Van Gogh paints PAUL GAUGUIN'S ARMCHAIR (see. p. 43). One finds loneliness even here. An unreal presence in space. Violent brushstrokes slash the purple colored chair. Two books and a candle speak of the owner's absence.

A few days before we parted, when illness forced me to enter an asylum, I tried to paint 'his empty place'. It is a study of his armchair of dark, red-brown wood, the seat of greenish straw, and in the absent person's place a lighted candlestick and some modern novels.[18]

Their drama culminates the evening of December 23, 1888. The two artists have a violent argument. Van Gogh delivers his severed ear lobe to a prostitute in Arles, of whom little is known. We will later explore this last subject.

The Gardener's Eyes

During his brief winter stay of 1885 in Antwerp, van Gogh writes to Theo explaining that the use of models is the quickest way for him to progress as a painter:

However, I'd rather paint people's eyes than cathedrals, for there's something in the eyes that isn't in the cathedral - although it's solemn and although it's impressive - to my mind the soul of a person, even if it's a poor tramp or a girl from the streets, is more interesting.[19]

The Church at Auvers, Auvers-sur-Oise, c. June 1, 1890, Museum d'Orsay, Paris 74x94 F 789

Tree Roots and Trunks, Auvers-sur-Oise, c. 25 July, 1890, van Gogh Museum, Amsterdam 50,5x100,5 F 816

This same sentence, I posit, could be read with an opposite meaning. "Given that I may not always have the chance to paint live models, I will therefore paint life into the inanimate". It is a recurring theme that he names in his own writing during his first year of painting:

I feel more and more as time goes on that figure drawing in particular is good, that it also works indirectly to the good of landscape drawing. If one draws a pollard willow as though it were a living being, which it actually is, then the surroundings follow more or less naturally, if only one has focused all one's attention on that one tree and hasn't rested until there was some life in it.[20]

CHURCH OF AUVERS is one of the last works painted by van Gogh in Auvers-sur-Oise just a few weeks before his suicide. It is a modest structure that he transforms into a gothic cathedral. Typical of his style, the church is a presence, so very expressive and foreboding as to become absolutely animate. It dramatically straddles a crossroads: the woman on the left, with her back turned to us, is life passing by while, on the right, the graveyard represents death. Death for him signifies a return to the earth. Its portent is thus personified in TREE ROOTS AND TREE TRUNKS (p. 29), a painting that may have been his very last.[21]

After his Christmas 1888 collapse, van Gogh is discovered by the police in his bed half alive, bleeding with his ear lobe sliced off. He is rushed to the hospital, the wounded ear is treated and he is released on the 26th. The very next day he undergoes his first break-down from his mental illness.[22] It is surely triggered by stress, fatigue, his abuse of alcohol and tobacco and his utter failure to realize his dream of a collective studio in Provence. Van Gogh exhibits symptoms of a strong neurosis. He is interned and released on January 7th and returns to painting.[23] At this time he suffers a second episode of hallucinations. The Dutch painter is now derided by the townsfolk. They laughed at him. He is chased on his outings by the local children who throw stones at him. Van Gogh officially becomes the town outcast. The Yellow House, that had formerly been his house of dreams, is now a barricaded fortress. Stones are thrown at it. Its windows are broken. Of course, van Gogh reacts. What ensues is a petition by the townsfolk declaring him a dangerous

madman and demanding he be kept in isolation. A fully cognizant Vincent is then tied up and incarcerated. By May 1889, after residing fourteen months in Arles, he voluntarily commits himself to the asylum hospital at Saint-Paul-de-Masusole in Saint-Rémy; less than 20 miles from Arles. His momentous Arles period ended and will become etched in the history of Painting. At Saint-Rémy, Vincent alternates between agonizing mental crises and long periods of lucidity. These moments of clarity are supremely creative and from them a slender thread of hope is re-born.

Van Gogh paints the unforgettable PORTRAIT OF A PEASANT in September of 1889. The peasant, probably a hospital orderly and gardener who accompanies him on his painting excursions, is a man that lives in nature and manifests nature itself. He is simultaneous with his environment; radiating his life force. The portrait exudes an unforgettable energy, a veiled smile, which is present in the face that moves to the clothes and from the clothes to the background, from the background to the hat and returns to the eyes in a circular vortex.

If a cathedral is capable of having eyes and thus a human presence, then within human beings there exists the full realm of the universe.

Portrait of a Peasant, «The Gardener»,
Saint-Rémy-de-Provence, September
1889, Galleria nazionale d'arte
moderna, Roma 61x50 F 531

The Sun of the Night

Popular lore imagines van Gogh as the painter of the bright yellow sun and dazzling light. If one revisits his paintings with open eyes, one not only calls up his sunflowers but also his famous THE PLAIN OF LA CRAU. Here is a symphony of yellows, flattened into overlapping parallel planes whose juxtaposition evokes depth without the use of perspective lines. This painting of a field vibrant with life is a hybrid of both a Japanese landscape and the sun bathed Provencal plains. However, if one reflects on all his production a new fact emerges. Van Gogh is as much a painter of the sun as a painter of the night. Indeed darkness, in his night paintings, has never before been so vividly filled with colors and meaning.

Vincent has painted evening colors in an extraordinary number of works from the very start of his career. [24]

Parsonage at Nuenen by Moonlight, Nuenen, November 1885, Private Collection 41x54,5 F 183

The Potato Eaters, Nuenen, c. 20-28 April, 1885, van Gogh Museum, Amsterdam 114x82 F 82

The Plain of La Crau, «The Harvest», Arles, c. 10 June, 1888, van Gogh Museum, Amsterdam, 72,5x92 F 412

The Café Terrace at Night, Arles, c. 12 September, 1888, Kröller Müller Museum, Otterlo 65,5x81 F 467

The Nigh Café, Arles, c. 7 September c. 1888, Yale University Art Gallery, New Haven 70x89 F 463

The night in his early works is pitch black, dark, rustic and romantic. This is seen in the painting of PARSONAGE AT NUENEN with his father's house and his small annex beside it, both emerging from the shadows. Housed in these dark rustic homes, especially the poorest, is the supper table of the THE POTATO EATERS.

The modern night of the town, and the evening in Arles are depicted in a com-

pletely different way. This is a night filled with a thousand phosphorescent colors created by the gas lights of the street. Night in these paintings is no longer the dark earth but rather the tumultuous life of modernity.

Let us study the setting of THE CAFÉ TERRACE ON PLACE DU FORUM. Van Gogh paints this scene from life while wearing a hat crowned with candles. The night scene is filled with "artificial" colors.

The use of the adjective - *artificial* - is key towards understanding van Gogh's exploration of color use. Of course, the colors on the café exterior are artificial due to gas lamps. These lamps illuminate a chrome yellow soffit, which in turn lights up an orange sidewalk platform and bounces off the cobblestones in orange, blue, and ocher. The light renders the large door frame Prussian blue, the walls of the houses lilac and the sky a cobalt blue with white flower-like stars. Van Gogh's color sensibility is consistently artificial, even when he is painting in full daylight. It is his tenacious pursuit of the artificiality of color that emphatically marks his role in the history of post-impressionist painting. In this early stage of Modernism, in the late nineteenth century, painting must be simultaneously analytical, scientific, abstract and above all "artificial". Seurat has a strictly scientific and anti-naturalistic approach to color theory and investigates through optics. In some paintings Cézanne tends to suppress color and gives precedence to the mechanical deconstruction and analytical study of objects. Gauguin, preferring a dream-like interpretation of painting, employs color in an autonomous and ornate manner. Van Gogh, in his turn, passionately explores the effects of complementary colors and color intensities to evoke an inner expression from objects. Van Gogh's color, and that of post impressionist painters, must be employed against convention; in this anti-naturalist and artificial manner.

Night is also the realm of mystery, where our fears can manifest. He writes upon painting THE NIGHT CAFÉ IN THE PLACE LAMARTINE in Arles:

My dear Theo,

Thank you a thousand times for your kind letter and the 300 francs it contained — after some weeks of worries I've just had a much better one. And just as worries don't come singly, nor do joys, either. Because actually, always bowed down under this money problem with lodging-house keepers, I put up with it cheerfully. I'd given a piece of my mind to the said lodging-house keeper, who isn't a bad man after all, and I'd told him that to get my own back on him for having paid him so much money for nothing, I'd paint his whole filthy old place as a way of getting my money back. Well, to the great delight of the lodging-house keeper, the postman whom I've already painted, the prowling night-visitors and myself, for 3 nights I stayed up to paint, going to bed during the day. It often seems to me that the night is much more alive and richly colored than the day. Now as for recovering the money paid to the landlord through my painting, I'm not making a point of it, because the painting is one of the ugliest I've done. It's the equivalent, though different, of the potato eaters. I've tried to express the terrible human passions with the red and the green. The room is blood-red and dull yellow, a green billiard table in the centre, 4 lemon yellow lamps with an orange and green glow. Everywhere it's a battle and an antithesis of the most different greens and reds; in the characters of the sleeping ruffians, small in the empty, high room, some purple and blue. The blood-red and the yellow-green of the billiard table, for example, contrast with the little bit of delicate Louis XV green of the counter, where there's a pink bouquet.

The white clothes of the owner, watching over things from a corner in this furnace, become lemon yellow, pale luminous green.[25] *[...]*

In my painting of the night café I've tried to express the idea that the café is a place where you can ruin yourself, go mad, commit crimes.[26]

Let us move on to another subject. Van Gogh finds himself at the Asylum of Saint-Rémy. On February 22, 1890 he makes a trip to nearby Arles. He relapses again into his illness upon returning and remains bedridden through the month of April. It is not until May that he returns to painting; creating eight works before leaving Saint- Rémy for his next stop. Among the works is his LANDSCAPE WITH COUPLE WALKING AND CRESCENT MOON. This too is a nocturnal composition. The man portrayed is, without doubt, himself. He is red-bearded, red-haired and wearing his famous worker's smock. The couple is not embracing but simply side-by-side. The woman points up to the sky while he holds a hand toward the ground.[27]

Van Gogh continues to suffer more and more mental depressions and in this time describes the painting of the tree in the garden at Auvers-sur-Oise:

This dark giant - like a proud man brought low - contrasts, when seen as the character of a living being, with the pale smile of the last rose on the bush, which is fading in front of him.[28]

If this tree is a metaphor for himself then, who is the fading rose he has painted?

Addendum

What an abundance of pain, mystery and hidden messages Vincent has left us! Perhaps, however we must speak of the most important and mysterious one. Let us step back and review once more the bedroom we previously visited. View it in detail, with our full attention and reflect on its minutiae. The table holds small grooming objects. They are a hair brush with other items... pillows, chairs, and paintings on the walls... This masterpiece of art hides a series of mysteries and clues. Let us pursue these clues by imaging what Vincent's might have written to his brother at this time:

The Garden of the Asylum, «*The Tree and the Rose*», Saint Rémy, c. October 30, 1889, Folkwang Museum, Essen, 73,5x92 F 660

Arles, February 4, 1889

My dear Theo,

Yesterday I mailed you a long letter which made reference to my returning to find the girl who witnessed my first nervous breakdown on December 23. This event created my permanent rupture with Gauguin and accelerated his departure. I believe that this is the time to tell you the full story of my crisis with Gauguin and the moment is arrived for you to know the full truth. Gauguin and I lived nine weeks of fertile creativity that was superhuman. You yourself know how much I produced and experimented in that time together. I tried to share with Gauguin what I was seeing, the places I loved, and we often painted there together. Each with our own vision. I am unsure if he was able to see a little of what I did or if my vision was able to influence his. On my part, I tried to assimilate Gauguin's way of thinking about paint and his capacity of imaging dreams and thoughts detached from reality.

I painted, among other things, that picture of Mother and Wil in the garden of Etten's presbytery. I also tried other paintings that were based on his work and his vision. But, our personalities gradually clashed. I felt that to Gauguin, my ambition, to make the little yellow house a studio collective, was nothing more than a romantic's dream. It also became clear to me that Gauguin, with his pragmatic and cynical nature, which sometimes reminded me of his having been a stockbroker and businessman probably accepted our invitation to Arles more for the alliance with you, as a means to sell his works, than with me as an artist and peer. Despite this, as you already know, I often humiliated myself for him, in my sincerest appreciation of his great art, by acting the role of a novice. In any case, Theo, I will affirm that together we did produce a strong series of works. I will venture to bet that in the future, this collaborative studio time in the yellow house of Arles will interest many.

However, beside the superhuman effort of painting, you should know that we pushed our bodies to the limit. We ate very little and in an irregular manner. We smoked tobacco and drank enormous quantities of absinthe which, consumed in large doses, produces myriad hallucinations. We were gradually worn down in both body and mind. You know that I am stubborn and do not back down from my convictions. Although I always wanted to respect Gauguin as a great master, I simply could not lie to myself and tell him that I admired the same painters he did such as Rafael or Ingres. He instead hates Monticelli and mocks Millet. This caused so many arguments. This was especially acute after our infamous trip to Montpellier to see Courbet. Rather than being a happy reunion, it turned into another source of friction and exacerbated our difference of opinion on art.

In addition to arguments over the art of the masters, our clashes extended to our own works. We diverged, in particular, on my own methods of painting. It became a constant humiliation of my paintings; with myself humbling the very things I love. The fact that Gauguin's paintings were selling well in this time and mine were not did not help either. Despite the excess of smoking and drinking absinthe, there was also the brothel here in our little Arles... Gauguin is a devourer of women; even more than Milliet. He uses them with malice and contempt.

Theo, I could not write you these details, my dear brother. How could I? How could I explain this after my unfortunate two years with Sien in The Hague? Remember how many misfortunes, betrayals and worries she had caused me? After my long history of disappointments with cousin Kee, with Ursule, Margot who caused me to suffer and the torments of Agostina in Paris, how could I tell you that I had fallen in love with Rachel? Rachel's profession, like Sien's, is in a brothel. She is a young girl who was kind to me and from that kindness we became linked. She was a person I was close too and despite the circumstances I felt bound to her.

A thousand things are connected to last Spring's flourishing of my paintings... see how many of my compositions show couples arm-in arm as they walk the fields of Arles. Do you understand, dear brother? It was a small sign of the deep blossoming of my heart. I believed, Theo that I saw myself in that couple walking, alone and against the world's adversity, in a dream that must not be denied any man.

You will ask me what Rachel has to do with this... She is very much part of it too, dear brother. A large part of my illness and the split with Gauguin is around her...

I was in the yellow house; in Gauguin's room. Gauguin was packing his bags and making ready for his departure. We were smoking and drinking rivers of absinthe, both of us mentally and physically exhausted with the impending finality of departure and goodbye. At some point, Gauguin and I found ourselves in another heated debate. In my despair at his leaving, I shouted in anger at him. Gauguin replied that I was an ignorant character and a naïve. He told me that my love for Rachel was the very proof of my naivety as well as a weakness of my character. Despite my replies, he insisted that Rachel was nothing more than a prostitute that he had taken to bed. He continued with details I will not bring myself to write to you. Theo! I became blind with rage. I regret it bitterly now. I wish I could regret all my past sins for this but; I was blinded by fury. I went to my room and seized my razor on the bedside table! Dear God, how did I do this, think it, and believe it for a second? May God forgive me! I was truly beside myself. I might have endured all Gauguin said but his cruelty toward Rachel I could not bear. I charged him while slashing my razor. Gauguin blocked me using his athletic strength by grabbing both my wrists. He blocked the one wrist bearing the razor along with its companion. In this lock we began a violent fight. I pushed hard with both arms while he blocked me with all his strength and bent my arms back; bringing the razor towards my face. In this manner, the razor neared my ear and, pushed by Gauguin; it sliced my left ear lobe, releasing a heavy jet of blood. We both froze in horror but the sight of the blood brought us back to our senses. Gauguin immediately left with his things, choosing to stay that night in a hotel until the next morning's train. I was now alone, despairing with my sliced ear lobe in my hand. I was overwhelmed by what had just happened and having to admit the utter failure of my project. (It was possible! It was not a dream!) You and I both believed we had a chance, with Gauguin and especially for

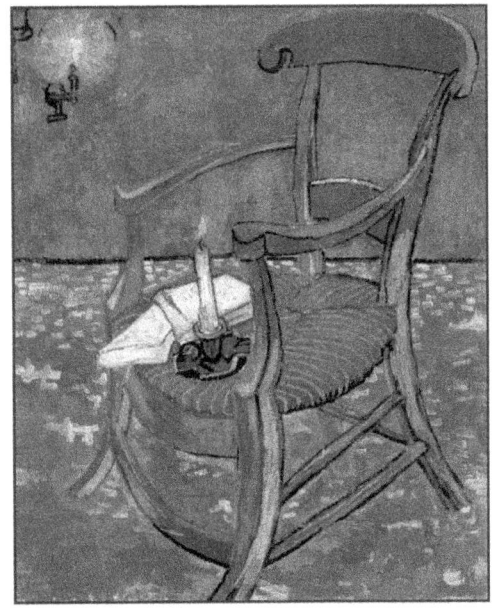

The Yellow House, Arles, c. September 28, 1888, van Gogh Museum, Amsterdam 76x94 F 464

Reconstruction of the Yellow House in Place Lamartine, Arles in Druick 2001

Gauguin's Armchair, Arles, c. November 17, 1888, van Gogh Museum, Amsterdam 72x90,5 F 499

me. What would you have done with a bleeding ear and severed piece that perhaps could be reattached? I did the only thing that seemed right at the time to protect myself and Gauguin's reputation. Imagine... I could have reported him it to the police. But this would have involved my friend in a painful criminal charge in which I too was guilty. The facts pointed to me even more than to him. I could have gone to the hospital, even in my dazed state... Surely the staff would have alerted the police who might have guessed at the truth? The only thing I could perceive clearly in my despair was Rachel. I needed to speak with her to tell her of my torment. Somewhere, I remembered having read that the Japanese give their beloved pieces of their fingers as a token of their love! I found my way to her in the night with the ear lobe wrapped in a piece of paper. Yes, I know it is the act of a madman but it is the only end. Rachel was occupied by a client at the brothel. When I was able to speak with her, I entrusted the package to her stating that is was precious and to keep it in her custody. She fainted in shock and I ran home more distraught than before. She came to the house at dawn found me bleeding to death and ran to the hospital to get help. The police accompanied the hospital staff because the blood clearly showed it was an act of violence, but they saved my life. Since then, dear brother, the truth has been far from what I dreamed of. Dear brother, in my fallen state, I could not tell you the truth. Perhaps I have become insane, perhaps a madman but it is part of my work and the absolute passion for it perhaps makes me risk all for it, including my own sanity. Ever yours,[29]

Vincent

The Inquiry

The fictional letter of February 4, 1889 was written by me with the intent of unraveling a complex ensemble of facts. It is based however on a series of verifiable facts and data confirmed by researchers.

My letter is apocryphal, but it is not unlikely that a letter of this nature really did exist and it was simply expunged.[30] It may also be possible that van Gogh explained this version of the truth to his brother during his visit to Arles December 25, in the aftermath of the tragedy. In either case, what I wish to underline is the factual reliability of the sequence of events that are described in the letter. Let us study the facts. Vincent writes a letter to Theo on February 3, 1889:

> Yesterday I went back to see the girl I went to when I went out of my mind. I was told there that things like that aren't at all surprising around here. She had suffered from it and had fainted but had regained her composure. And what's more, people say good things of her.[31]

Let us also review the event as described in the local paper in Arles.

Local News

> Last Sunday, at half past 11 of the evening, an individual named Vincent van Goug (sic), painter – of Dutch origin, appeared at the House of Tolerance n. 1 and requested to speak with a Rachel to whom he entrusted ... his ear stating: "Guard this precious object". He then disappeared. After being informed of these actions that could only be of a madman, the police went to the individual's home the next morning, where they found him lying almost lifeless on the floor. This unfortunate was admitted to urgent care at the hospital.[32]

This December 30th article from the local newspaper is perhaps lacking information and not altogether accurate however, two facts emerge. First, there is no mention of self-mutilation and second, there is a direct quote from Rachel. It seems reasonable to me - other authors will likely agree this point[33] – that the young woman played a role in the tension between Gauguin and van Gogh. Vincent wrote about this point a decisive and very clear phrase to Bernard:

With Gauguin, blood and sex have the edge over ambition.[34]

The tension with Gauguin is certainly motivated by numerous and burdensome reasons. Rachel may have represented the classic "straw that broke the camel's back", which is my hypothesis. It is possible, given the sequence of events... the call for help, documented in the seemingly insane gesture of a madman to give her an amputated earlobe. This episode should be read combined with various factors. One technical factor is obvious. The earlobe could have been re-attached but. However van Gogh chose not to go to the hospital at that time for fear that the fight would be discovered, implicating both Gauguin and him in a crime. Another factor is psychological. The severed ear lobe represents to van Gogh a token of his love for Rachel, the product of a bloody struggle sparked by his defense of that love.[35]

Gauguin and Theo's role

I believe there exists little doubt around the details of the physical event that caused the amputation. Let us review the factors. The first one, that makes my re-construction plausible, comes from a simple exercise. Grasp a spoon with your left hand,(since a razor is too dangerous), and try to attack a stronger person who has blocked you by grabbing your wrists. Simulate the struggle to stab in this blocked position. The push-back from your opponent will easily lead to the scenario I have described. This being: the razor's blade comes in contact with your left ear, slicing it due to the resulting backwards and forwards movement of pushing back!

A second factor supporting this hypothesis is the "official" reconstruction of the event as described by Gauguin. It is a patently implausible description the event but within it one can spy some shreds of truth. Gauguin describes it in detail for the «Mercure de France» in the October 1903 article[36] entitled *Avant et Après*. The synopsis of his description is adopted by almost all books as well as a famous film,[37]

> On the afternoon of 23 December 1888, van Gogh would have chased his friend Gauguin, (who at the time was his

guest), down the street with a razor blade, cursing him and attacking him when Gaugin turned to face him. Once home, while Gauguin was in a hotel awaiting his departure from Arles the next day, van Gogh, in the throes of hallucinations, cut off half of his left ear, wrapped it and gave it to a prostitute in the brothel he used to frequent with Gauguin and then went home to sleep. He was discovered there the next morning by the police and immediately hospitalized until his release on January 7, 1889. [source is Italian Wikipedia, but please note that this is Gauguin's version in *Avant et Après*].[38]

Gauguin is truthful in stating that van Gogh attacked him with a razor blade. However, Vincent was obviously not deterred by his friend turning to face him nor did he return home to slice off his ear as an act of self-mutilation! Gauguin proffers a version of events that completely absolves him of any responsibility. The extraordinary fact is that his reconstruction of events omits four fundamental details. What are these four details and what is the proof they are omitted? Herein lies the proof. Gauguin himself relays these details, and does it a few days later in a letter to their common friend Émile Bernard. [39] Let us scrutinize this.

Gauguin writes to Bernard that the afternoon of December 23, van Gogh has said the following to him:

«"So, you are leaving" And when I answered "yes", he tore a piece of newspaper entitled "the assassin disappeared" and pressed it in my palm.»[40]

This episode indicates, without a shadow of a doubt, that the principle reason for their tension is Gauguin's departure. Why would Gauguin omit this in is his official declaration? The reason is obvious. His departure is an accusation of his betrayal of the collaborative studio in the Midi. Vincent has articulated it through his metaphor of the fleeing assassin. It is not convenient for Gauguin to mention this detail, since it would reveal that his own actions are the primary cause of their argument. Gauguin makes no mention of this in *Avant et Après*. His omission in the article makes as the argument never existed. Instead, he takes great pains to underscore that van Gogh showed various signs of mental instability.

There are two other omissions in Gauguin's version of the event, that may be even more important. He writes:

I thence spent the night in a hotel and when I returned home all of Arles was in front of our house. The police arrested me, because the house was covered in blood. This is what happened. [41] [His version follows of the "madman's" amputation which is subsequently used].

Let us return to this version of the events as described by Gauguin in his letter to Bernard. The most important detail, that was obviously censored in *Avant et Après*, is that *Gauguin was arrested*. The reason behind his arrest is obvious. The furious fight between the two in the house, must surely have been heard by neighbors. The house was situated close to other homes on the town square of Arles and even the police station was nearby. So, Gauguin fled to a hotel and is arrested by the police upon his return home the next morning. How could they not arrest him?

The third is the bloodied house. This lends further proof to my reconstruction of the events. The struggle occurs in the Yellow House. The logical explanation for blood throughout the house would be a continued scuffle while the ear was bleeding. If one self-mutilated one's ear, it would not be so clear as to why «the house was covered in blood».

The fourth detail, which carries incredible weight, is that the letter to Bernard *makes no mention at all of Theo's role*. The story depicted by Gauguin is as though Theo were not present at all and had absolutely no role in the matter! There is surely a strong motive for this omission. Let us understand the reason by revisiting the sequence of events after Gauguin's arrest. Gauguin asks to send a telegram to Theo as soon as he is brought to the police station. The police send the telegram. Naturally, Gauguin does this not only to communicate Vincent's situation to Theo but also *because he hopes Theo can arrange his release*. Theo arrives in Arles the morning of December 25th via the overnight train from Paris. The train station is adjacent to the police headquarters and, since Gauguin called him, Theo spoke with Gauguin before reaching Vincent at the hospital in the center of town.[42] Theo sorts through his brother's version of events, analyses the facts and comes up with the version of a self-mutilation. There are a a good reasons for this choice. Firstly, it is partially true - for the initiator of the attack is Vincent, Secondly, the criminal involvement of Gauguin in the story does not help anyone or help to solve anythin. Finally, Theo has a contract with Gauguin that gives him exclusive rights to the profitable sale of his works.⁴³ This self-amputation version is provided to the police by Theo as though it were Vincent's. The version frees Gauguin from custody. A released Gauguin returns to Paris with Theo on the same night, December 25th. It is surprising that no one to date has linked these facts from the many sources available.

My reconstruction also includes another aspect of the history that would otherwise remain incomprehensible. Van Gogh's letters following the tragedy of December 23rd contain no harsh reference to Gauguin, neither in letters to Theo nor in letters to Gauguin. Gauguin, in turn, is never harsh towards Vincent. The reason is precisely because they are mutually responsible for the amputation of the ear and it is not to the advantage of either of them to uncover the episode.⁴⁴

The reality of life

Van Gogh's relationship with Rachel is another chapter in this history. The relationship was much deeper than previously thought.⁴⁵ Here are some facts. Van Gogh writes to his brother on March 16th 1888, when he assisted the police in the investigation of a crime committed at the door of the local brothel. It was an argument resulting in two deaths:

> *I took advantage of the opportunity to go into one of the brothels in the little street called 'des Récollets'. Which is the limit of my amorous exploits vis-à-vis the Arlésiennes.*⁴⁶

A clue emerges from this letter. It relates the violent climate surrounding the world of prostitution. It is also a premonition of his future quarrel with Gauguin. The letter confirms that van Gogh entered the brothel on March 12th; which is the date of the murders. It is plausible that he met Rachel on this occasion or possibly on another visit in subsequent days. Rachel is also named in the local paper and specifically by Vincent in his previously cited letter of February 3rd.

Van Gogh visited Arles at least four more times after his departure. His first visit was in mid-July 1889 followed by a second towards the mid-November, the third at end of January 1890 and then another in May 1890; before returning to Paris. It seems very likely that he returned to the brothel to meet with Rachel.[47] Van Gogh returns to the clinic in Saint-Rémy completely distraught from the January 1890 visit. He plunges into one of his longest and worst depressions. These trips are confirmed by witnesses, despite the evidence of self-censorship on the issue. They are relevant to an understanding of the relationship between Vincent and Rachel.

However, this alone is not enough and we turn to the paintings for further proof of their link. Shortly after his March 1888 visit to the brothel where probably meets Rachel, Van Gogh has a personal blossoming of creativity and joy. He produces many paintings of flowering orchards with various versions of the Pont de Langlois. In earlier years he had written to his brother:

> Not that I shall become anything extra-ordinary, but "ordinary"; and by ordinary I mean that my work will be sound and reasonable, and will have a right to exist, and will serve some purpose.
> I think that nothing awakens us to the reality of life so much as true love. And whoever is truly conscious of the reality of life, is he on the wrong road? I think not. But to what shall I compare that peculiar feeling, that peculiar discovery of love? For indeed when a man falls seriously in love, it is the discovery of a new hemisphere.[48]

That van Gogh has discovered this new hemisphere is evident and is symbolized in detail in the extraordinary series of works from his Spring of 1888. (See p. 21). The bridge of Langlois is, in particular, a subject Vincent approaches very romantically. In a letter to Émile Bernard, also dated March 18th, he describes the theme thus:

> At the top of this letter I'm sending you a little croquis of a study that's preoccupying me as to how to make something of it — sailors coming back with their sweet-

hearts towards the town, which projects the strange silhouette of its drawbridge against a huge yellow sun.[49]

One of these studies described by van Gogh, perhaps the very first, was ruined. He omits the fact though, that he kept a small part for himself; which currently resides in Oslo. (See p. 1). This small painting shows a couple walking arm in arm. The two figures have distinctive features worth noting. The man wears a yellow straw hat (exactly like the one van Gogh usually wore and with which he portrayed himself in self-portraits). If this were not enough of a clue, the man also dons the blue workman blouse that van Gogh adored and wore as his symbol of the working-man painter. Could it be plausible that the figure represents not only a sailor but a generic effigy of the painter himself? Is it truly a big leap of the imagination? It seems to me that from van Gogh's point of view, the man in the fragment is himself. The beautiful young woman beside him is dressed in a vibrant red and has long fair hair, (red here), pinned up on her head. In my opinion, it is very important that the characters in the paintings represent both the painter and Rachel. After all, van Gogh went to the trouble of saving this fragment from the larger work instead of simply painting over it as he did others. Whether they actually represented Vincent and Rachel is not so critical; it simply is as if they did. In the following months at Arles, Vincent continues to paint lovers in his landscapes. They appear strolling in wheat fields and in the town park holding hands. (See p. 79). There are two works in which they wear the same clothes Vincent was typically seen wearing.[50]

Iman, Rachel and the secrets of the bedroom

Let us now turn our attention to a series of details worth deciphering in the bedroom in Arles. On October 16, 1888, van Gogh sends his brother his first sketch of the painting (See p. 52). Two portraits are depicted on the wall. The portrait by the window appears masculine while the other is a woman with a fringe wearing a shawl (See detail a p. 54). There is a new portrait above the headboard of what is probably his mother that he had just completed based on a photograph. The next day he sends Gauguin a letter. The sketch in this letter is modified. The portrait of his mother above the head board is omitted. It has been substituted with the theme of a tree. The walls again show both male and female portraits. (See detail b p. 54). The subsequent oil painting reveals one more change (See p. 24). This time two male portraits appear on the wall. One is of his close friend Lieutenant Paul-Eugène Milliet (See p. 55), a great seducer of women and the other is of the Belgian painter Eugene Boch, representing the figure of a poet (See p. 54). They obviously signify his ideal of love (both sensual and spiritual) present within a room. As we previously noted, he also parallels this theme of an ideal pairing by composing objects in sets of twos, (two portraits, two chairs, two pillows).

Note that this painting retains no trace of the women. The ideal of love is evoked more subtly with the two male portraits on the wall rather than with a direct representation.[51] Let's look at the "details" of the paintings for further clues. Artists are famous for hiding messages within their details that are decipherable only to a few. To the best of my knowledge, a study of these hidden clues has not been previously explored. The following are my observations.

The painting of the Arles bedroom had been damaged.[52] Van Gogh wished to retouch it but Theo suggests that he make a copy. Van Gogh receives the original during his internment at Saint-Rémy and makes the copy (See p. 54-55). Let us review what changes occur. The portraits of Boch and Milliet disappear from the walls. They are replaced, instead, by a recent self-portrait paired, most extraordinarily, with the portrait of a woman! (See detail f p. 55). Let us examine this last portrait closely. It depicts a red-haired woman of delicate features with her hair pinned up about her face. Can there be any doubt that, after all the previous events, he has placed next to his own self-portrait an image of his beloved, Rachel?

If a doubt does exist, then allow me to offer a rebuttal. Van Gogh painted a smaller version of this same picture, to send to his mother and sister Wil in Holland. (see Back cover). The two portraits on the wall are changed once again! This time he pairs his self-portrait with the portrait of a dark-haired woman (See detail d p.

Sketch of the Bedroom, Letter to Theo, October 16, 1888 L. 705

The Bedroom, Detail of the night-table, See entire painting p. 24 F 482

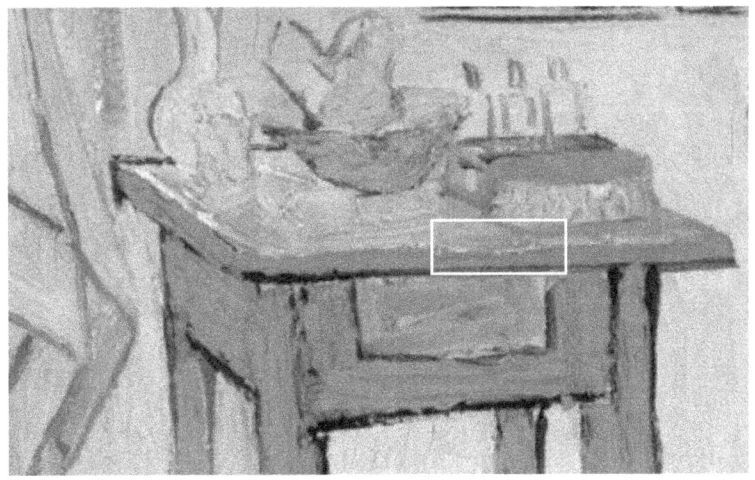

53). It is likely a portrait of Wil. The domestic setting of the composition has been tailored to suit his mother and sister, rather than be an intimate and personal one for himself.

The razor blade

I describe the events of the tragic night in my letter. It begins during Gauguin's final preparations for departure. His packing must have required an extended period of time given the amount of works he had painted over a period of nine weeks. I describe van Gogh's fetching the razor blade from the night table. A razor blade is never mentioned in any of the descriptions of the room; some of which are extremely detailed.[53] However, upon careful observation of the painting, one can see it clearly on the night table!

This same razor blade is shown in the original painting of October 1888. It is understandable that he censured the wretched weapon out of the later versions of the painting![54] Theo writes to his sister shortly after Vincent moves out of their shared home in Paris:

> It is not easy to replace a man like Vincent. He has many acquaintances and a very distilled understanding of the world. I am convinced that, given one more year, he will make a name for himself. He is part of a lineage of pioneers of ideas that become lost in the mundane life of daily living and thereby lose their brilliance. He also has a good heart and is always applying his efforts for others benefit. Too bad for the individuals who do not wish to know and understand him.[55]

a.

b.

c.

d.

e.

a. Detail of the sketch in the letter to Theo, October 16, 1888
b. Detail of the sketch in the letter to Gauguin October 17, 1888
c. *The Bedroom*, Detail See Entire entire p. 24 F 482
d. *The Bedroom*, «For the Mother» detail, Saint Rémy, September 1889, Museum d'Orsay, Paris 56.5x74 F 483 See Back cover
e-f. *Vincent's Bedroom* detail, entire painting p. 54–55 F 484

Portrait of Eugene Boch, «The Poet», Arles, c. September 2, 1888 Museum d'Orsay, Paris, 45x60 F 462

Portrait of Lieutenant of Zouaves Paul Milliet, «The Lover», Arles, c. September 25, 1888, Kröller Müller Museum, Otterlo, 49x60 F 473

Vincent's Bedroom with Self Portrait and Feminine Figure, «The Bouquet», Saint Rémy, c. September 1, 1889, Art Institute, Chicago 73x92 F 484

55.

Madame Roulin, «La Berceuse», Arles, c. 23 December 1888, January 22, 1889 Museum of Fine Arts, Boston 72x92 F 508

Icons

Let us return to the larger scope of his work. Failure in art can sometimes explain the reasons and motives of the resulting works. Van Gogh, on that infamous night of December 23, had a painting on his easel. It was the portrait of MADAME ROULIN, the wife of his dear friend the socialist postman Joseph Roulin. He had painted him several times as well as members of his large family including young Armand, the Camille boy and the baby Marcelle. This painting is also titled LA BERCEUSE, the lullaby. Van Gogh produces five versions of it. It is therefore a very important painting, showing through its previous unsuccessful versions, exactly what Van Gogh was seeking.

> *So I must tell you it, and you can see it in the Berceuse, however failed and weak that attempt may be. Had I had the strength to continue, I'd have done portraits of saints and of holy women from life, and who would have appeared to be from another century and they would be citizens of the present day, and yet would have had something in common with very primitive Christians.*[56]

This note renders van Gogh's intent clear. He is striving to create icons. The letter points to the primitivism in his paintings, - " ...and who would have appeared to be from another century" - , his search to be more real than reality and his struggle to give life to what is represented. Incredibly, van Gogh succeeds in this endeavor with the painting of the room, the chairs and the sunflowers in the room. His desire to succeed is explicitly strong and evident in La Berceuse. Perhaps another quote, from a different context, helps one fathom this further. Vilém Flusser writes:

> The universe of traditional imagery, not yet muddied by theory, is a world of magical circumstances. It is a world of the eternal recurrence of oneness, in which everything lends meaning to another and everything is given meaning by the other: it is a world full of signs and of gods. Through this world full of signs, man lives an environment of circumstances. This is what determines the life of the imagination: *all is pregnant with meaning and all needs to be brought to harmony.* The life of guilt is determined by sins.[57]

This is a good example to reflect upon. Van Gogh breathes life into things because therein lays the contradiction of his art. That is his challenge. This life cannot be but magical. Evoking life itself brings it into being. It becomes our lives, it lives within us. This is the way to grasp the environment, history and life by experiencing it every day and living it to its end. It is a world dramatically rendered peaceful. His bedroom is the ideal example where, he insists a thousand times, he wishes to convey a presence of absolute peace. He infuses life into objects because therein lies the contradiction; his artistic motive.

Flowers

If there exists a painting, that fully reveals the terrible knot between life and death, hope and the search for unattainable happiness, it is the picture van Gogh painted in early February 1889 Branches of an Almond Tree in Blossom; just a few months before his death. On January 31st, Theo and Jo announce to Vincent the birth of their son, giving it the name Vincent. A new and unexpected Vincent van Gogh now exists. Here comes a new arrival following the footsteps of the gravestone and the painter himself. Van Gogh patiently paints a yearning picture that gives tribute to life. It is a tribute to the child's life and the happy couple, Theo and Jo Bonger, his sister-in-law. The painting is for their bedroom.

Let us examine this work. Enter the leaves, observe the colors, follow the petals and it leaves no doubt. Vincent brings these flowers to life, as he did his Bedroom, his Sunflowers and the Still-life with Bible. This new life however and the painting are his sentence themselves. Can he continue to economically impose on Theo with the new arrival of his nephew and the responsibilities it carries for his brother? He suffers an acute crisis of depression while painting this work but after a week returns to his work. He travels to Arles on the 19th, sees Rachel and returns with one of his longest and worst nervous break- downs. By May, he is interned in the asylum. He then travels to Paris to visit the young couple and meets the infant. He settles in an inn at **Auvers-sur-Oise, a rural village near his doctor just twenty miles from Paris**. In that stay he is able to paint stunningly beautiful paintings and drawings. It is a final hymn. On July 27th he shoots himself. [58]

Vincent dies shortly thereafter in the arms of Theo. In September, Theo, and Jo and organize an exhibition of Vincent's works in their home with the help of Emile Bernard. The house fills with painter friends, critics and the works are displayed the way he had wished them to be seen. During the art opening, Theo has a terrible crisis and enters a trance. He too is rendered insane by pain. He dies in February at age 34; just six months after Vincent The great adventure of bringing van Gogh's work to the world lies in the hands of Jo, his sister-in-law, and with his namesake nephew. Life wins over death. That life of Vincent with Theo is with us and becomes ours.

Branches of an Almond Tree in Blossom, Saint Rémy, c. 1 February - February 18 c. 1890, van Gogh Museum, Amsterdam 73x92 F 671

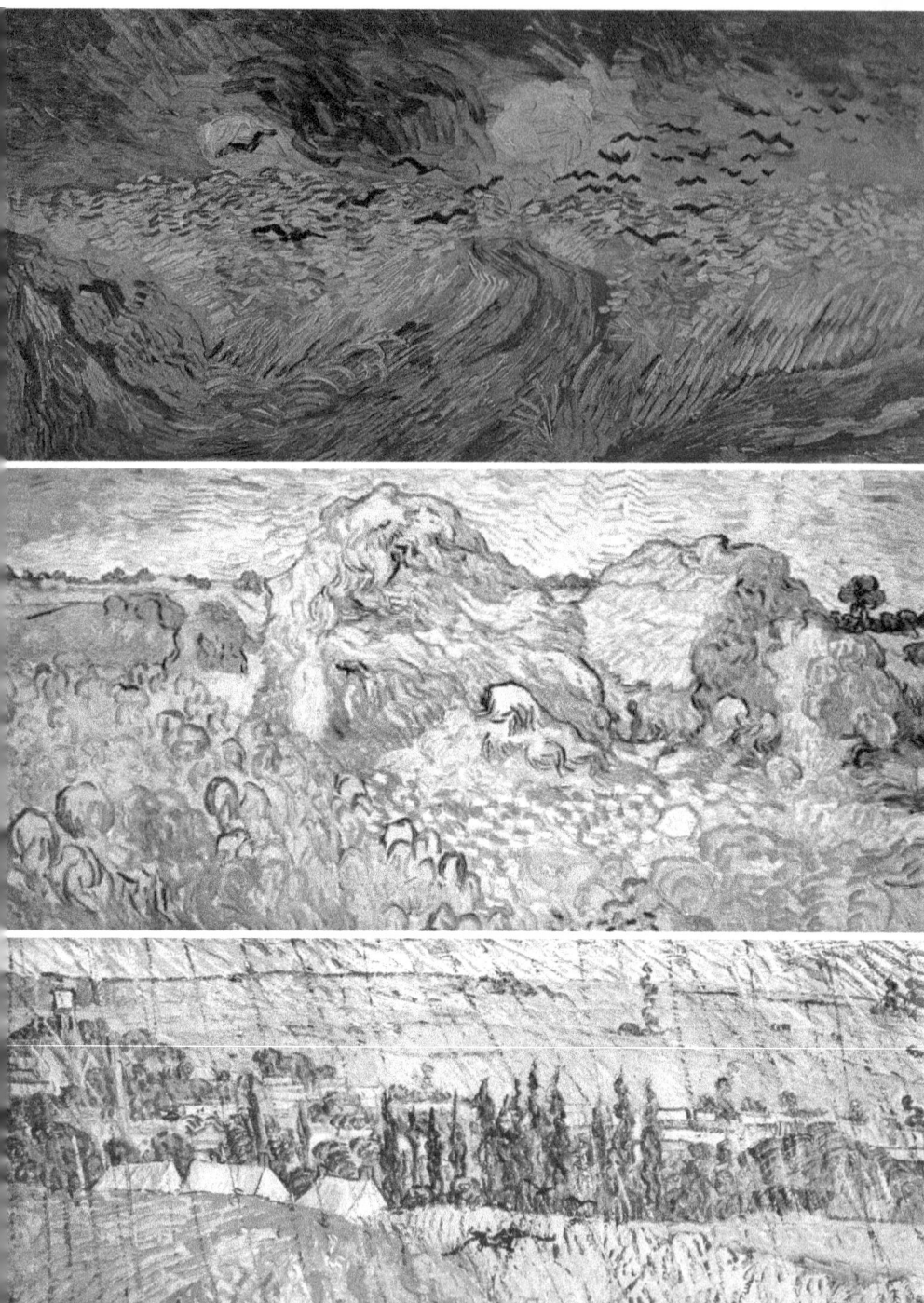

60.
Wheat Field with Crows, Auvers-sur-Oise, c. July 8, 1890, van Gogh Museum, Amsterdam, 50x100 F 779

Wheat Field with Stacks, Auvers-sur-Oise, July 1890, Foundation Beyeler Riehen, Basel, 50x100 F 809

Landscape in the Rain, Auvers-sur-Oise, c. July 1890, National Museum of Wales, Cardiff, 50x100 F 811

Sheaves of Wheat, Auvers-sur-Oise, July 1890, Museum of Art Wendy and Emery Reves Collection, Dallas, 50x100 F 771

Wheatfields, Auvers-sur-Oise, c. June 23, 1890, Österreichische Galerie Belvedere, Vienna, 50x100 F 775

Wheat Field Under a Clouded Sky, Auvers-sur-Oise, c. July 9, 1890, van Gogh Museum, Amsterdam, 50x100 F 778

Daubigny's Garden, Auvers-sur-Oise, c. June 20 1890, 50x101,5 F 777

Thatched Cottages by a Hill, Auvers-sur-Oise, July 1890, Tate Gallery, London 56x51.5 F 793

Landscape with the Chateau of Auvers at Sunset, Auvers-sur-Oise, c. June 18 1890, Art Museum, Cincinnati, 50x100 F 770

Chronology of events [59]

1852
March 30: a baby, called Vincent Willem van Gogh, is stillborn in Zundert;

1853
March 30: Vincent Willem van Gogh is born in Zundert;

1855
February 17: His sister Anna is born;

1857
May 1: Theodorus (Theo) is born;

1859
May 16: His sister Elisabeth (Lies) is born;

1862
May 16: His sister Willemina (Wil) is born;

1864
October 1: He attends school in Zevenbergen;

1866
September 3: He attends high school in Tilburg;

1867
May 17: His brother Cornelius (Cor) is born;

1868
March 19: He returns to live at home;

1869
July 30: Vincent starts an apprenticeship with Goupil&Cie, The Hague.

1873
June 13: He takes up work at the London branch and falls in love with Ursule Loyer;

1875
May 15: He is transferred to the Paris branch. Ursule rejects his marriage proposal;

1876
April 1: He resigns from Goupil&Cie;
July 1: He becomes an assistant preacher in Isleworth (England);

1877
May 9: He begins his studies for the entrance exam toward a university degree in theology.
July 30: He abandons his studies.

1878
August 23: He travels to Lacken (Belgium) to attend the Evangelical College;
December 26: Vincent leaves for Borinage, where he is hired short-term as an evangelical preacher

1879
July 30: His term is not renewed but he continues to preach as a volunteer in Cusmes (near Borinage);
1880

August 20: He decides to become a painter and dedicates his time to his art with the moral and economic support of his brother, Theo;
October: He relocates to Brussels where he visits a fellow Dutch painter van Rappard;

1881
April 12: He moves back to Etten, meets with Theo and stays at his parents' home; that summer he falls in love with Kee Sticker but is rejected by her;
December 31: he relocates to The Hague where his cousin Anton Mauve gives him painting lessons;

1882
February: He forms a romantic relationship with Clasina Maria Hoornik ("Sien") who becomes his model.
April: he cuts ties with Mauve;
July 15: Sien moves in with V. along with her daughter and newborn.

1883
September 11: He leaves Sien and moves to Drenthe;
In December, he returns to his parents in Nuenen;

1884
March: He signs an artist/dealer contract with Theo;
August; Margot Begemann falls in love with V. and she attempts suicide because her family forbids her from marrying him;

1885
March 26: His father Theodorus suddenly dies;
November 27: He leaves Nuenen for Antwerp
1886
February 28: Vincent moves in with Theo in Paris

1887
March 2: He curates an exhibition of Japanese woodcut prints at the Café Tambourin. He has a romantic relationship with Agostina Segatori which ends in July;
November: He organizes an exhibition in the Restaurant du Chalet in Montmartre on Avenue de Clicky, also known as le Petit Boulevard. The show includes works by Anquetin, Bernard, Arnold Koning, Toulouse-Lautrec and others;

1888
February 20: V. arrives in Arles;
March 10: He writes to Theo describing in detail his idea for a collective artist studio (the Atelier du Midi);
March 18: he writes to Bernard describing his painting of the draw bridge. His relationship with Rachel probably begins at this time;
May 1: He rents the Yellow House which he arranges as a studio while lodging in a boarding house above a café;
June 6: He visits Tarascon and from the 10th to the 16th of June he stays in Saintes-Maries-de-la-mer;
September 17: He moves into the Yellow House;
October 23: Gauguin arrives at five in the morning;
December 21: Theo writes Vincent of his engagement to Johanna Bonger;
December 23: Vincent and Gauguin quarrel;
December 24: Gauguin is arrested; Vincent is hospitalized for an amputated left ear lobe;

December 25: Theo arrives in Arles, visits his brother and arranges for Gauguin to be released from custody;
December 26: Vincent is released from the hospital;
December 27: He suffers a nervous attack and is newly interned at the hospital;

1889

January 7: V. is released from the hospital;
February 3: V. visits Rachel and writes to Theo of it;
February 4: V. falls into a second nervous crisis and is interned for ten days;
February 25: thirty local townspeople pass a petition that forcibly hospitalizes him. He is fully rational and it is done against his will;
March 23: Signac visits him and together they enter the yellow House that has been cordoned off by police; in the following weeks, V. is outdoors during daylight hours but returns to sleep in the hospital at night;
April 17: Johanna Bonger marries Theo;
May 8: Vincent voluntarily admits himself to the asylum of Saint-Paul-de-Mausole of Saint-Rémy-de-Provence;
July 14: He makes a trip to Arles;
July 16: He falls into a deep depression that lasts for two months through the month of August;
December 24: he undergoes another nervous crisis that lasts approximately one week;

1890

January 18 or 19: He returns to visit Arles;
January 19 or 20: He has a nervous crisis lasting through January 31;
January 31: Theo and Johanna's son Vincent is born;
February 1: He probably undergoes another attack that leaves him debilitated for another week;
February 10: He writes to the critic Albert Aurier; in response to the publication of the first article ever written on his work;
February 22: He suffers one of his worst crises, a crisis that lasts up to eight weeks;
May 16: He leaves the asylum and most probably travels to Arles;
May 17: He arrives in Paris to join Theo, Johanna and the baby; he visits with friends and sees his paintings again;
May 20: He moves to Auvers-sur-Oise, to be closer to Dr. Paul Gachet;
June 8: Theo, Jo and the baby visit Auvers and meet Dr. Gachet;
July 6: visits Theo in Paris;
July 27: Vincent shoots himself with a gun;
July 29: Vincent dies at dawn;
Towards the end of September, Theo, assisted by Emile Bernard, mounts an improvised retrospective exhibition of his brother's works in Theo's apartment.
October 9: Theo collapses into a catatonic state from the final stage of syphilis and is hospitalized;

1891

January 26, 1891 Theo dies.

Trees with Ivy, «*Lovers' Hides*», van Gogh Museum, Saint Rémy, 20 May, c. 1889
47x67 F 1522

Annotated Bibliography

FAILLE 1928 - F Jacob, Baart de la Faille, *L'Oeuvre de Vincent van Gogh. Catalogue Raisonné*, 4 vol. G. van Oest, Paris e Brussels, 1928.

This is a monumental work of the scholar from Antwerp. It is the first catalog of Van Gogh's entire works with later editions. The edition of 1970 was edited by Abraham Hammacher and the most recent in English has been published by Alan Wofsy Fine Arts, San Francisco 1992. The citation «F» followed by a number refers to this specific catalog and is also a useful device to easily locate the works on the internet. A useful website is www.vangoghgallery.com

VAN GOGH 1959 - *van Gogh complete Letters*, 3 volumes, with introduction by Johanna van Gogh-Bonger (English edition New York Graphic society based on 1953-1953 Dutch Edition of the Centenary of the birth).

For many decades, this source has been the indispensable reference of all van Gogh scholars and remains a reading of unsurpassed density of information. Today, after fifteen years of preparation, this edition is superseded by van Gogh 2009.

ELGAR 1958 -Frank Elgar, *van Gogh*, Fernand Hazan, Paris 1958.

A well-written and dense text that persuasively links the life and works of the artist. It remains relevant to this day.

TRALBAUT 1969 - Marc Edo Tralbaut, *Vincent van Gogh*, Edita, Lausanne, Lausanne 1969.

I recommend this book to any person wishing to begin a serious study of van Gogh. It is suitable for all ages and for any reader. Tralbaut is a considerably scientific scholar; who during his post Second World War research, even managed to track down witnesses alive at the time. The book interweaves a highly detailed biography, with the reading of the works. He offers innumerable ideas and suggestions. I give personal thanks to this author, who in my boyhood, first revealed Vincent to me.

LECALDANO 1971 - Paolo Lecaldano, *L'opera pittorica completa di van Gogh*, 2 volumes, Rizzoli, Milan 1971.

The catalogue is largely based on the complete works of art historian J-B de La Faille 1928. It is well organized despite the limitations of an edition for the general public.

HULSKER 1980 - JH Jan Hulsker. *The Complete van Gogh*, Phaidon, London 1980.

This is the last edition of the complete oeuvre. It is undoubtedly the art historical authority, and extremely useful to the study of the individual works.

STEIN 1986 - Susan A. Stein, *Van Gogh A Retrospective*, Park Lane, New York 1986.

An invaluable source with innumerable historical documents, otherwise difficult to find.

LEEMAN 1988 - *Vincent van Gogh* (with essays by A. Monferini, R. de Leeuw, et al) De Luca, Rome 1988.

Catalogue of the 1988 exhibition in Rome, the first in Italy for many years, with extensive plates.

LEYMARIE 1989 - Jean Leymarie, *Van Gogh*, Skira, Newton Compton, Rome 1989.

A flawless essay, precise and complete with an original weaving of full disclosure and scientific soundness.

BONAFOUX 1989 - Pascal Bonafoux, *Van Gogh Self portraits*, Artline Editions, Paris 1989.

A comprehensive publication of van Gogh's self-portraits with a critical anaylisis of them regarding the artist's biography.

VAN UITERT 1990 - Evert van Uitert, Louis van Tilborgh, Syraar van Heugten, *Vincent van Gogh. Paintings*, Arnoldo Mondadori, De Luca Edition, Milan and Rome 1990.

It is a good publication for its editing and excellent reproductions, but it is disappointing given the exhibition's exceptional cultural context. The exhibition was held at the centenary of the artist's death in the van Gogh Museum of Amsterdam. The curators prefer a philological approach of study and analysis primarily comparing different versions of the same work and the difference between *Tableau* and *Etude*.

VAN DER WOLK 1990 - Johannes van der Wolk, Ronald Pickvance, E. B. F. Pey, *Vincent van Gogh. Drawings*, Arnoldo Mondadori, De Luca Edition, Milan and Rome 1990.

Careful examination of the drawings with a detailed history and a catalogue with accurate reproductions of the artwork shown in the exhibition of the centenary of the Kröller Müller Foundation from Otterlo.

WALTHER 1990 - Ingo F. Walther and Rainer Metzger, *Vincent van Gogh All the Paintings*, Taschen, 2 voll. Køln, 1990.

This is the first volume that publishes more than 90% of the paintings in color. It is extremely helpful in this regard. The essays are very detailed in incorporating aspects of literary criticism with known facts about the painter.

TILBORGH 1999 - Louis van Tilborgh, «"Les Religions passent, Dieu Demeure"», in *Millet van Gogh*, Editions de la Réunion del musées nationaux, Paris 1998.

An excellent and accurate essay. This writing is from the very best school of art historians.

DRUICK 2001 - Douglas Druick, Peter Kort Zegers *Van Gogh and Gauguin. The Studio of the South*, with essays by B. Salvesen, K. Lister, M. Weaver, Thames & Hudson, London, 2001.

This outstanding work pairs with an equally stunning exhibition. These two authors have put together perhaps the best book on van Gogh. They offer amazingly accurate, extensive and illuminating references, detailed day by day, including the actual weather data, the relationship between Gauguin and van Gogh in Arles, as well as invaluable pages on the events preceding and following the development of the two painters.

HOMBURG 2001 - Cornelia Homburg, *Vincent van Gogh and the Painters of the Petit Boulevard*, Rizzoli, New York 2001.

The catalogue of a beautiful exhibition. Several of the essays explore a little known phase of van Gogh's two years in Paris: Vincent's role as curator in the exhibition that brought recognition to the painters of the so-called Petit Boulevard in reaction to the first generation of Impressionists. Among other things, it is clear that V. took on the role of a talent scout which became invaluable to his brother who himself admitted to not having this aptitude.

CHILDS 2001 - Elisabeth Childs, «Seeking the Studio of the South. Van Gogh, Gauguin, and Avant-Garde Identity» in Homburg 2001.

An interesting and detailed essay.

GOLDIN 2002 - *L'impressionismo e l'età di van Gogh* (Marco Goldin ed.), Linea d'ombra, Conegliano 2002.

Handsome volume with a large section on van Gogh with valid contributions indicated in the footnotes.

MARCHIONI 2007 - Nadia Marchioni, *Van Gogh e il postimpressionismo*, Education.it, & Il sole 24 ore, Florence 2007.

The text presents a broad critical essay that is a well-organized and updated compendium of the many essays written up to the date of publication. It also includes a bibliographical essay.

GOLDIN 2005 - *Gauguin van Gogh. L'avventura del colore nuovo* (ed. Marco Goldin), Linea d'ombra, Conegliano 2005.

The catalog is well made and enjoyable to read, with accomplished essays some quotes of interest cited.

STOLWIJK 2005 - «"Per una buona causa" Théo van Gogh e Paul Gauguin», in Goldin 2005.

The relationship between Theo and Gauguin is studied here in detail and was useful to me in building some aspects of my thesis.

VAN HEUGTEN 2008 - *Van Gogh and the colors of the night*, (eds. S. van Heugten, J. Pissarro, C. Stolwijk), MOMA | van Gogh Museum, New York 2008. The exhibition has the merit of having brought to light a very important aspect of the works of van Gogh.

VAN GOGH 2009 - *Vincent van Gogh – The Letters, The Complete Illustrated and Annotated Edition*, (eds. Leo Jansen, Hans Luijten, Nienke Bakker of the Van Gogh Museum in association with the Huygens Institute), VI vol., English edition, Thames and Hudson, London 2009, French edition Actes sud, Paris 2009.

This magnificent edition has long been awaited. It is an exemplary art historical work, full of valuable references and annotations that make it easy and enjoyable to read including a plethora of correspondence organized chronologically. It includes the works of art van Gogh admired in detail and numerous references to the literature of the period. The Van Gogh Museum generously shares this enormous scope of work with the public. Their website http://vangoghletters.org/vg/ is perhaps the most referenced about an artist and is a complex tool for scholarly investigation. Among many things, it allows targeted searches in the database through a highly effective search engine. One can access high resolution images of all the original letters with built-in links to relevant artworks and literature referenced in the correspondence.

HOMBURG 2009 - *Vincent van Gogh. Campagna senza tempo - Città moderna* (ed. Cornelia Homburg), Skira, Milan 2010.

A well-written catalog of an exhibition that, while not presenting the peak of van Gogh's artistic career, was extensive and well organized by referencing the works of the painters who inspired him. I make particular reference to the curator's essay entitled «Rappresentare città e campagna».

Endnotes

¹ Fictional letter which I propose as plausible. I began studying van Gogh passionately in 1970. I read all his letters twice over as a young man and avidly collected postcards, prints and books of his work. I even painted and I looked to him, like many, as a standard by which to try. I am grateful today that, at 55 years of age, fortune has given me the opportunity to write this little book. The more I reflect on the path ahead or the beginning from which to untangle the works (and life), the more I think about the transcendentalism of Frank L. Wright, Emerson and Thoreau. Start with a few basic premises, a few principles that motivate your whole being and then all that is left is the making. Van Gogh handwriting is designed by J.C. Renner with some of my modifications.

² Credit is due here to John Allen's lecture "History as Inquiry" given at the Institute of Ecotechnics, Santa Fe, NM, in October of 2010.

³ Giulio Carlo Argan, *L'Arte Moderna 1770-1970*, Sansoni, Florence 1970 p. 161. The singular verb, "becomes", is a minuscule seed, the tiniest imaginable, which allowed the approach described in this book to germinate. This intuition was not elaborated further by the great art historian, but it was enough. Of course there exist many profs of this tendency toward personification. Van Gogh tends to self-censor this theme, but it will increasingly become manifest, particularly in his period at Saint-Rémy. See Homburg 2010 p. 32.

⁴ I have briefly referenced this in *Architettura e Modernità*, Carocci, 2010 (pp. 40-41):

Today's objects speak for themselves. The world and its things are no longer subject to human rules but rather, to their own internal logic. It creates a radical reversal. The vision of the Renaissance placed the observer at the center of the world, (as found in the rules of perspective - the picture plane, the vanishing points and the points of measurement make up a design based a world projected centrally onto the human retina). Today's objects are independent of human eye. Cézanne's paintings begin, even from the vantage point of aesthetic sensibility, to engage the autonomous "existence" of the object; irrespective of the observer being there to observe.

The key word of this new mode of vision is analytical. This means two absolutely essential concepts: the first is that each object has its own shadow, its own independent point of view (often "Isometric"), and its own "arbitrary" color; (although the latter has implications, especially in the research of two other contemporary painters - Gauguin and van Gogh who engaged in a violent intellectual battle over the meaning behind this new need for the arbitrary.)

Both van Gogh and Cézanne render the object autonomous, but they do this via opposite directions. Cézanne does it through mechanics and the hyper analytic rendering of the object. Van Gogh does it via personal projection onto the object; transforming it through a method of hyper personification. Gauguin had already perceived this personification in van Gogh's oeuvre and called him a "romantic" for it.

Couple walking between rows of poplar, (detail), Auvers, c. 22 June 1890, Cincinnati Art Museum, Cincinnati 50x100 F 773

⁵ Immediately after his father's death, van Gogh painted a watercolor of this composition, and included it with a letter to Theo. The oil painting was made a few months later, shortly before his final farewell of the family home. He will never see his mother or sisters again during his lifetime. His placement in the composition of the book *Joie de Vivre* vs. the Bible, brings to mind Vittorio Cigoli's observation:

> Vincent is simultaneously, an opponent and a supplicant: he desires to impose himself and "his" logic and is at the same time in dire need of his father's blessing. («Nostro fratello Vincent. Alla ricerca della personalità» in Goldin 2002 p. 382.)

Cigoli focuses on the figure of the psychoanalytic "addiction" and in this light reinterprets a passage from a letter to Theo dated June 22-24, 1880. See van Gogh 2009 p. 249. On this topic, I must add a comment.

His father, the pastor Theodorus van Gogh lent support to his son several times; physically, morally as well as financially. This occurred under various circumstances: for example, he went in person to bring home a debilitated Vincent from Borinage and again, bringing him back home from Brussels. This "paternal" role of help and support was progressively taken over by his brother even while their father remained alive. An example of this early shift was when Vincent was admitted to the hospital in The Hague in June 1882 and the brother went to visit and assist. Theo steps into this role completely upon the death of their father.

There is a fact worth emphasizing here: both the brother and the father are named Theodorus! This namesake is a further confirmation to Vincent that their roles *are one and the same*: Theo is not the younger brother to be protected rather, he is the father figure that cares for him. Son and father create together and build together. He articulates this attitude in his last letter, never sent, but found on his person on July 29, 1890. I leave in the French original:

> mais pourtant mon cher frère, il y a ceci que toujours je t'ai dit et je te le redis encore une fois avec toute la gravité que puissent donner les efforts de pensée assidument fixée pour chercher à faire aussi bien qu'on peut – je te le redis encore que je considérerai toujours que tu es autre chose qu'un simple marchand de Corots, que par mon intermédiaire tu as ta part à la production même de certaines toiles, qui même dans la débâcle gardent leur calme. (Letter to Theo dated July 23, 1890 in van Gogh 2009 vol. 6 p. 326 «...Through me, you have your part in the actual production of certain canvases which, even during my crisis, keep their calm.»)

⁶ Uitert 1990 p. 54 and Druick 2001 pp. 6-9 examine this canvas in great detail and Tralbaut 1969 highlights a strong link to his father's death based on psychiatric literature and the artist's mixture of guilt, (for their contentious relationship), and sense of loss at his father's passing. Van Gogh utterly censures the symbolic meaning of the painting when he writes to his brother. He describes the work strictly in terms of its relationship to a Manet's painting. Despite this, he also underlines that it was quickly painted «in one day» and alludes to its parallel to the speed and suddenness of his father's death. (Letter to Theo van Gogh dated c. October 28, 1885 in van Gogh 2009 vol. 3 p. 324). Once again a confrontation is revealed in his discussion of painting technique with his brother, (who had suggested he lighten his color palette, while van Gogh stubbornly continued to pursue "local color" in this phase of his production).

⁷ The tombstone, for the good fortune of life to the infant Vincent, does not bear the exact same date of birth which for Vincent and his dead brother is of March 30 for them both.

[8] Van Gogh will write that symbolically the tower will perish like all buildings, (its partial demolition began in 1885), but not the idea of religion that it embodies. The old church is discussed with precision by Tilborgh 1999. It is interesting to note that the medieval building, will become an isolated object (because the small village is eventually relocated elsewhere) and it will be left incomplete (the existing church will never be fully rebuilt). The symbolic power of the image as a self-portrait is underscored by another story. Van Gogh does not send one of the paintings of the tower to Theo, but instead gives it to his neighbor Margot Begemann, who will attempt suicide after falling in love with Vincent.

[9] Druick 2001 p. 75 recalls the paintings of Millet's clogs and points to the urbanity of the shoes by Vincent, while Tralbaut 1969 p. 203 focuses on the psychological value of the subject. Form as a condensed memory is a thesis presented in detail in Michael Leyton, *Shape as Memory*, Birkhäuser, Basel 2005 from the book series The IT Revolution in Architecture with my preface entitled «History».

[10] The same is noted in the postscript by Homburg 2010 p. 251.

[11] Anquetin, Bernard, Koning, Toulouse-Lautrec and van Gogh showed works in the exhibition of the Petit Boulevard. This interior may also simply be that of several other restaurants that van Gogh painted in Paris. He painted for example, the restaurant Rispal (F 355), and the Sirens (F 313, F 312) both in the Asnières quarters, or Chez Bataille (F 1392) in Montmartre where he went almost daily with his brother and compatriot André Bonger, Theo's future brother in law. However, in none of these restaurants had van Gogh organized a major exhibition as is revealed in this painting by the exhibition announcement and a painting on the wall.

[12] Letter to Gauguin, October 3, 1888 in van Gogh 2009 vol. IV p. 304.

[13] F 370, AGOSTINA SEGATORI SITTING IN THE CAFÉ DU TAMBOURIN, Paris, February 1887 is the most well-known. The nude is F 330. There may be others. The portraits where the model is generally identified as Agostina are F 367 and F 381.

[14] Letter to Theo, July 23-25, 1887 in van Gogh 2009 vol. III pp. 367-368.

[15] Letter to Theo, October 16, 1888. See van Gogh 2009 vol. IV p. 330 Vincent writes: «The walls are of a pale violet. The floor is of red tiles. The bedstead and the chairs are fresh butter yellow. (...) The doors lilac. And that's all - nothing in this bedroom, with its shutters closed. The solidity of the furniture should also now express unshakeable repose. (...) The shadows and cast shadows are removed; it's colored in flat, plain tints like Japanese prints.» His letter to Gauguin of the following day, (Van Gogh 2009 vol. IV p. 332) resumes the description of the changing aspects of some details. The floor is no longer «red brick» but «a broken and faded red (...) and among which the only white is the little note given by the mirror with a black frame (to cram in the fourth pair of complementaries as well).» And ends as a sort of promise: «we'll talk.» He includes a sketch for Gauguin, presumably more advanced, showing an outstanding change to which we will return.

[16] Letter to Theo, September 23, 1888 in van Gogh 2009 vol. IV p. 281.

[17] Letter to Theo, September 26, 1888 in van Gogh 2009 vol. IV p. 288.

[18] Letter to Albert Aurier, February 9, 1890 in van Gogh 2009 vol. V p. 198.

[19] Letter to Theo, December 19, 1885 in van Gogh 2009 vol. III p. 331.

[20] Letter to Theo, October 12-15, 1881 in van Gogh 2009 vol. I p. 294.

[21] It has long been believed that his last painting is the famous WHEAT FIELD WITH CROWS (F 779). Hulsker1980 indicates that SHEAVES OF WHEAT (F 771) is the last work, while Lecaldano 1971 indicates TREE TRUNKS AND ROOTS (F 816) as the last painting. There exists no certainty in any of the three cases but there is agreement that F 816 is among the last works made. The appearance of ten canvases, in last month of his life, painted in the highly elongated horizontal format of 50x100 cm brings to mind a searching for a more intimate contact with the earth.

[22] According to recent studies, his illness would be a manic-depressive or bipolar neurosis perhaps related to his having syphilis, though syphilis has never been fully confirmed. A recent essay that incorporates several other current studies on the disease is by Vittorio Cigoli, «Nostro fratello Vincent. Alla ricerca della personalità» in Goldin 2002 cit. Also see Bruno Guerri for the issue of insanity in his *Follia? Vita di Vincent van Gogh*, Bompiani, Milan 2009.

[23] See the section «Chronology of Events» pp. 63-65 for a detailed listing of dates tracking the different mental crisis van Gogh undergoes. They all tend to coincide with his trips to Arles while he is treated at the asylum in Saint Rémy.

[24] The New York MOMA recently curated a splendid exhibition on this theme, cit. op. van Heugten, 2008. I also reference two other major exhibitions (and their catalogs) organized by the Metropolitan Museum in New York and curated by Ronald Pickvance *Van Gogh in Arles* (1984) and *Van Gogh in Saint-Remy and Auvers* (1986).

[25] Letter to Theo, September 8, 1888 in van Gogh 2009 vol. IV. p. 258.

[26] Letter to Theo, September 9, 1888 in van Gogh 2009 vol. IV. pp. 262.

[27] See Goldin 2002 «A symbolic language solely through color». Goldin among other things, focusses on the fact that «of all the paintings at that time, [«Couple walking on a crescent moon», The Stroll is one of the few that is not even mentioned to Theo; perhaps because the painting reflected his deepest desires» p. 347.

[28] Letter to Émile Bernard, November 26, 1889 in van Gogh 2009 vol. V p. 148.

[29] The letter is fictional but the facts are faithfully reconstructed.

³⁰ Johanna Bo Bonger, Theo's wife, who conserved the correspondence between the brothers, removed some letters from the first edition. In particular, they were removed from the Nuenen period in which the two brothers had a friction. The expunged letters reappeared in the 1953 edition honoring the centenary of his birth. See van Gogh 1959.

³¹ Letter to Theo, February 3, 1889 in van Gogh 2009 vol. IV p. 408. It is worth noting the woman's desire to reassure Vincent, arguing that such oddities are commonplace. Vincent underlines that she suffered very much of the episode of that terrible night « ... and had fainted». Then there is a logical jump «... it says a lot of good for her.» The rest of the letter is extraordinarily clear. It is in these three sentences that ambiguities and omissions are gathered.

³² Weekly news bulletin from the *Forum Répubblicain,* December 30, 1888. The original can be found in various sources, among them, in Stein, p. 1986 131.

³³ Hans Kaufmann, Rita Wildegans, *Van Gogh Ohr: Paul Gauguin und der Pakt des Schweigens*, Osburg Verlag, Berlin 2008. Childs 2001 pp. 133-136 dwells at length on interpreting the act of bringing to Rachel the ear was an act of love from Japanese culture. This same theme is discussed in Armando Favazza, *Bodies under Siege: Self-mutilation and Body Modification in Culture and Psychiatry*, The John Hopkins University Press, Baltimore 1987.

³⁴ Letter to Émile Bernard, November 1, 1888 in van Gogh 2009 vol. IV p. 348.

³⁵ Childs 2001.

³⁶ Cited in several sources; among them Stein 1986 pp. 123-128.

³⁷ The 1956 Hollywood film "Lust for Life" directed by Vincente Minnelli and based on the 1934 novel by Irving Stone.

³⁸ Paul Gauguin, in Avant et Après in Stein 1986 p. 126-127 writes:

> I had already almost crossed Place Victor Hugo, when I heard behind me a familiar short footstep, rapid and irregular. I turned just at the moment when Vincent rushed towards me, an open razor in his hand. My look at the moment must have been powerful indeed, for he stopped, and lowering his head, took off running in the direction of the house. [...] Here what is happened. Van Gogh returned to his house and, immediately, cut off his ear close to the head. He must have taken some time in stopping the hemorrhage, for the next day they were many wet towels scattered about in the floor tiles of the two rooms downstairs. The blood had stained the two rooms and the little stair case that led up to our room.

Gauguin's version of events which became the official one in innumerable publications has enormous omissions, (most notably, the arrest of Gauguin and the presence of Theo!) and many strangely underlined details most notably the insistence on the presence of the blood in the house. There exist incongruities and errors. Van Gogh in fact is released by doctors on Dec. 26th for an ear injury. It is the on the following day, December 27, that he is hospitalized again - after suffering his first full-blown crisis - and is discharged on January 7, 1889. Moreover, being in police custody on the 24th, Gauguin most likely departed Arles on December 25, 1888. This is as also sustained by Druick 2001 p. 260.

[39] The letter has been reproduced in Druick 2001 p. 260. Bernard's letter dated January 1, 1889 is addressed to the critic Aurier but in it Bernard relates what Gauguin wrote to him. He does this by copying Gauguin's letter which uses the first person (Gauguin's words). There is no reason to believe that details I discuss might have been invented by Bernard.

[40] Ibidem. The omission of these marginal details is also a fact. It is also a fact that Gauguin's biased version of the events published as *Avant et Après* was unquestioned and retold over and over as if it was the truth.

[41] Druick 2001 p. 260. The authors credit the original source as the letter found in their 1985 edition I reference their note 284 on p. 392.

[42] There exists a record of the meeting between Theo and Vincent on December 25, 1888 in which Vincent blesses his brother's upcoming marriage though he recommends Theo to continue his mission of promoting art. Letter of Theo to Jo, December 28, 1888 cited in Druick 2001 under note 292 p. 392.

[43] Stolwijk 2005 provides details of Theo's growing admiration of Gauguin and of his successful sales of works by the painter. One of Theo's most important sales occurred just in the aftermath of Gauguin's arrival in Arles for some 600 francs (500 went to Gauguin almost € 5000 today). The contract between Theo and Gauguin for Atelier South was for 150 francs, more or less what he need to live on: See «The Financial Backgrounds» in vangoghletters.org/. It is difficult not to assume that Vincent was jealous of Gauguin's success. It was not so much Gauguin's financial achievement vs. his dismal commercial failure but because this was happening with Theo's help.

[44] Kaufmann 2008 cit. (Van Gogh's Ear: Paul Gauguin and the Pact of Silence, published in German and discussed in «Le Figaro», in an article and an interview published on May 4, 2009), offers a reconstruction of events that is different from mine. He argues that Gauguin cut the ear with the blow of his sword in front of the brothel. Leo Jansen, the director of the van Gogh Museum in Amsterdam along with curator Louis van Tilborgh refutes this version which obviously I do not even credit. In any event, even if the version by Kaufman 2008 is very doubtful; (even if a later letter from Gauguin to van Gogh shows him requiring a fencing mask and gloves, I agree with these authors that there "was a pact of silence" and Rachel, though not the only reason, had not played a secondary role in the explosion of December 23rd. I have never found any mention in existing sources of the role of Theo in the whole affair. Even in the recent books of Giordano Bruno Guerri, Follia? Vita di Vincent van Gogh cit. nor in the book by Martin Gayford, *The Yellow House: Van Gogh, Gauguin, and Nine Turbulent Weeks in Arles*, Penguin Books, London in 2006 nor in Druick's 2001 work, of which we have repeatedly referenced to the reader as the most reliable source. It is argued by Druick that almost certainly Gauguin left together with Theo on December 25th and it was Gauguin who told police to telegraph Theo. A letter is published in stating Gauguin «who was arrested», but Druick 2001 seems to support the argument of a self-amputation and does not focus on the role of Theo in resolving the scandal. Scholars, for whom I cannot emphasize enough my appreciation, have all the evidence on the table, and yet do not make the leap to connect the dots.

⁴⁵ In my research of the events, I soon hypothesized that Rachel played a decisive role. Her role was unexplored in the numerous publications I had read over the years. There exists however a very good and interesting novel, by the art historian Bundrick, faculty member at U. Florida in St. Petersburg, in which Rachel's role is anything but minor. See Sheramy Bundrick, *Sunflowers*, Avon, New York 2009. For the exhibition Cornelia Homburg curated in Rome in 2010-2011, she writes in the biography panels for the exhibit an illuminating introductory sentence. It is the first time that Rachel takes on a strong role:

WOMEN

For van Gogh, «Women are religion». At the time of his London stay, he was rejected by the daughter of the widow Loyer. Years later, following the marriage refusal of his cousin Kee Sticker, he burns himself with a candle flame until fainting from the pain. Vincent desires the image of a woman as his protector, a woman as mother. The prostitutes play an important role in his lonely life as a bachelor; such as Sien or Rachel to whom, on December 23, 1888, he delivers the ear following a violent argument with Paul Gauguin. They share a desperate despair with him and he feels the souls of these women as loving and close to him in a painful existence. Sien has scarred skin, probably from smallpox, and is afflicted with venereal diseases. Despite this, van Gogh admires her as a great tragic force and writes: «She and I are two unhappy ones hold each other's company and each other's burdens.»

I wish to emphasize, in this valuable commentary, that importance is given to Rachel, and the well balanced phrase «following a violent argument with Paul Gauguin in the December 23, 1888» which is exactly my thesis. Homburg also writes a beautiful essay «Representing the city and country», Homburg 2010, that discusses in depth the theme of the garden of love; a theme that van Gogh repeatedly confronts in Paris and in Arles and even during his time at the asylum in Saint-Rémy.

⁴⁶ Letter to Theo, March 16, 1888 in van Gogh 2009 vol. IV p. 26.

⁴⁷ Tralbaut 1969 p. 264 claims «Dr. Leroy, the director of the asylum Saint-Paul-de-Mausole in Saint-Rémy-de-Provence, said that Vincent had often visited this woman, in the company of Gauguin.»This quotation confirms the obvious, namely that Gauguin also had dealings with Rachel and certainly knew her. Indirectly it also confirms a conjecture, by the doctor from Saint Rémy, that one of the main reasons to make a day trip to Arles on January 19, 1890, and leave the asylum in Saint Rémy was specifically to visit with Rachel.

⁴⁸ Letter to Theo, November 7, 1881 in van Gogh 2009 vol. I p. 304. A section of this letter is referenced in Bundrick, *Sunflowers*, cit. In the section which I have added in, the connection between the knowledge of reality and that of love becomes very strong.

⁴⁹ Letter to Bernard, March 18, 1888 in van Gogh 2009 vol. IV p. 28. Bob Harrison on www.vggallery.com writes at length about this fragment.

⁵⁰ SUNSET: WHEAT FIELDS NEAR ARLES, end of June 1888, (F 465), LOVERS: THE POET'S GARDEN IV, October 1888 (F 485), and (F 474) and (F 479) see. p. 79. It is interesting to note that at least in paintings F 485 and in F 479 the clothing of the lover recalls the painter's own. The reference to himself becomes absent in the painting made after Gauguin's arrival in Arles.

⁵¹ «During the Autumn of 1888, van Gogh was seen as an uncertain and vulnerable lover, not only was he exposed daily to the spectacle of arrogance and dissolute success of Gauguin, but he also envied the sexual exploits of his friend Milliet, a Lieutenant of the Zouaves, whose military career was, from Van Gogh's opinion, enhanced by his success with women, while Van Gogh's occupation as a painter compromised him». Childs 2001. On Boch, as a witness of poetry and spirituality, this is what Vincent wrote: «Ah well, thanks to him - at last I have a first sketch of that painting I've been dreaming about for a long time - the poet. He posed for it for me. His fine head, with its green gaze, stands out in my portrait against a starry, deep ultramarine sky». Letter to Theo, September 3, 1888 in van Gogh 2009 v. IV p. 253.

⁵² On January 22, 1889 he writes that seeing his canvases again after his illness, the bedroom is his strongest. He sends the painting with the others to Theo on April 30th 1889, shortly before his admission to Saint Rémy. In a series of subsequent letters van Gogh writes of the damages sustained by the canvas and a variety of things for Theo to do, in particular the re-stretching of the works. (May 23, June 9). On October 21, 1889 he writes to his sister Wil «you will find the interior ugly, an empty room with a wooden bed and two paintings, but I painted it twice. I wanted to get an effect of simplicity, as in Felix Holt» (a character from a novel by George Eliot who lives in absolute simplicity). Then two other small clues but nothing further. In repeated descriptions of the room, an object is always missing: the paintings on the walls. Van Gogh describes everything except the pictures. And yet art has an enormous importance for a painter. Van Gogh painted a same size replica of the painting and writes of it to Theo on September 6, 1889 in van Gogh 2009 V p. 79. The new painting seems very loyal, a true copy, for it is significantly different. More writings later "never" emphasize the differences from the original. Van Gogh creates another copy of the room that he sends home in Holland to his sister Wil and his mother. This "copy" is smaller than the original and even here there is no mention of the changes. The last mention in the correspondence occurs when Theo gets both large versions of the room (the smaller was sent to Holland). Theo states that he prefers the second version and writes: «I've safely received your consignment of the Wheat field and the two Bedrooms. Above all I like the last one, which in terms of color is like a bouquet of flowers. It has a very great intensity of color.» Letter to Vincent of December 22, 1889 in van Gogh 2009 vol. V p. 169. Why this excursus? *There is never any mention in the letters of the change in some details*. Yet they are very important, of course; both obvious and hidden.

⁵³ For example, in the careful detailing of its site in the room. This is not uncovered in neither Druick 2001 nor in the reconstructed room shown in the video www.youtube.com/watch?v=cHhA-pk0CAw.

⁵⁴ I have dwelt this long on the details in order to help the reader grasp the most probable story that is condensed in my "plausible" letter of February 4, 1889. It is a new and hopefully convincing argument. Of course I am happy to have comments, or additional details about counter-evidence, at university antonino.saggio@uniroma1.it I can be easily contacted. Finally, a little mystery that I have left deliberately unresolved. Who's Iman? It is not difficult to find out, with today's technologies. But if you have difficulty, of course, I will inform you.

⁵⁵ Letter from Theo to one of the two sisters, written from Paris 1887, quoted in Walther 1990 p. 228.

⁵⁶ Letter to Theo, September 10, 1889, van Gogh 2009 vol. V p. 92.

⁵⁷ Vilém Flusser, *Immagini*, Fazi editore, Rome 2009 p.19. I owe my discovery of this book, which deals with the difference between electronic images and traditional images, to Roberto Sommatino whom I wish to thank. I also found a mention of this concept by Venturi, «the artist's soul has separated from his product, it is canceled from the subject and has made the object in itself beautiful, an image of worship» and «a vague premonition that the sun shining on the flowers maddens him, a faith in that piece of nature as if it were an idol, imparting character of art to the beautiful object.» in Lionello Venturi, *Sulla via dell'impressionismo*, Einaudi, Turin 1970 p. 315 and p. 321.

⁵⁸ «Love is indeed something positive, something strong, something so real that it's just as impossible for someone who loves to take back that feeling as it is to take one's own life.» Letter to Theo, November 7, 1881 in van Gogh 2009 v. I p. 303.

⁵⁹ The Chronology of events is created from Tralbaut 1969 and has been updated with the last 2009 edition of van Gogh's letters. I have provided the events that support the thesis of this book.

The Public Garden with a Couple Strolling, «The Poet's Garden», Arles, c. September 30, 1888, Private Collection

ITool Book Series

The Instruments of Caravaggio
Roma a-Venire
Quindici Studi Romani
Datemi Una Corda E Costruirò
The IT Revolution Thoughts On A Paradigm Shift
Five Masterworks By Louis Sauer
Urban Voids

First edition March 2011
Second edition July 2011

All right reserved on the text

Copy of this book can be bought at

http://stores.lulu.com/ninos

www.ingramcontent.com/pod-product-compliance
Lightning Source LLC
Chambersburg PA
CBHW031417040426
42444CB00005B/612